Confronting Empire

Praise for the First Edition

"[Eqbal Ahmad] was a shining example of what a true internationalist should be. . . . Eqbal was at home in the history of all the world's great civilizations. He had an encyclopedic knowledge of states past and present, and he knew that states had a rightful role to play. But he also knew that states existed to serve people—not the other way around—and he had little to do with governments, except as a thorn in their side. To friends, colleagues, and students, however, he gave unstintingly of himself and his time. . . . His example and his memory will inspire many to carry on his work."
—Kofi Annan, secretary-general of the United Nations

"A very dedicated and honorable activist, Eqbal was right in the middle of everything. . . . He was a student of revolution and imperialism and a very good one."
—Noam Chomsky, MIT

"Fighting words, wise words, from one of the most powerful activist intellectuals of our time."
—Gayatri Chakravorty Spivak, Columbia University

"For the thousands of people who have missed Eqbal Ahmad in the year since he died, this book comes like rain during a drought. In these interviews, we hear Ahmad's compelling voice again, musing over the Indian subcontinent, Algeria, the United States, and Palestine; recounting his encounters with Mahatma Gandhi and Yasir Arafat; fulminating against the West's pusillanimity over Bosnia and Kosovo; laying out his solution to the Kashmir conflict; and discussing his plans to found a university in Pakistan named after the Arab historian and sociologist Ibn Khaldun. Such is the range and breadth of David Barsamian's interviews, my only regret is that the book is not twice its length."
—Radha Kumar, Council on Foreign Relations

"Eqbal was a teacher, a poet-analyst, a mentor to far more of us than he knew."

—Phyllis Bennis, Insitute for Policy Studies

"These interviews provide a wonderfully focused, yet wide-ranging compendium of Eqbal Ahmad's worldview. . . . Ahmad was a courageous thinker and activist, an inspirational presence wherever progressives gathered, and a remarkable human being filled with love, humor, and generosity of spirit."

—Richard Falk, Princeton University

"Hearing Eqbal Ahmad's voice again, in these eloquent pages, renews one's sense of loss. The people of Bosnia and Kosovo, in particular, have been deprived of an ally when they need one most. But perhaps the voice can still unblock a mind or two, in this dull era of the parochial Left."

—Christopher Hitchens, *The Nation*

"With the voice of truth and compassion, Eqbal Ahmad weaves a tapestry of resistance—from Pakistan to Palestine, and Indonesia to Iraq. Ever challenging fanaticism and bigotry, particularly the scapegoating of Muslims and the demonization of Islam, Ahmad speaks for a vision of secular internationalism. *Confronting Empire* is a must-read for anyone concerned with issues of multiculturalism, liberty, and social justice."

—Zaineb Istrabadi, Columbia University

"We have here the ideal combination for a dazzling intellectual encounter: thoughtful questions by a superb interviewer, David Barsamian—and brilliant responses by the extraordinary Eqbal Ahmad, recorded just before Ahmad's death."

—Howard Zinn, Boston University

"Eqbal Ahmad was a multitude of men—scholar, activist, political analyst, teacher, diplomat, visionary—but, above all, a foot-soldier in the army of peoples everywhere."

—*Race and Class*

CONFRONTING EMPIRE

Eqbal Ahmad

Interviews with

DAVID BARSAMIAN

Forewords by

EDWARD W. SAID

AND PERVEZ HOODBHOY

Haymarket Books
Chicago, Illinois

© 2016 Eqbal Ahmad and David Barsamian
Foreword © 2016 Edward Said
Previously published in 2000 by South End Press (Boston)

This edition published in 2016 by
Haymarket Books
P.O. Box 180165
Chicago, IL 60618
773-583-7884
www.haymarketbooks.org
info@haymarketbooks.org

ISBN: 978-1-60846-621-4

Distributed to the trade in the US through Consortium Book Sales and
Distribution (www.cbsd.com) and internationally through Ingram
Publisher Services International (www.ingramcontent.com).

This book was published with the generous support of Lannan Foundation
and Wallace Action Fund.

Special discounts are available for bulk purchases by organizations and
institutions. Please call 773-583-7884 or email info@haymarketbooks.org
for more information.

Cover design by Rachel Cohen.

Printed in the United States.

Entered into digital printing February 2022.

Library of Congress Cataloging-in-Publication data is available.

Contents

ACKNOWLEDGMENTS

My gratitude goes to Edward W. Said for his foreword; Agha Shahid Ali for his translation of Faiz Ahmed Faiz's "Dawn of Freedom"; S. Farooq Ali for his Urdu calligraphy; to Julie Diamond, Urban Hamid, and Rebecca Kandel for photographs; Zoltan Grossman of the Wisconsin Cartographers' Guild for the map; and Zaineb Istrabadi, Zubeida Mustafa, and Emran Qureshi for their help with several of the references. Thanks to Eqbal Ahmad's many students, friends, and colleagues at Hampshire and elsewhere for their assistance and advice. Sandy Adler is the goddess of transcribers. Sonia Shah and Anthony Arnove at South End Press were a joy to work with in the editing process.

Interview excerpts appeared in *The Progressive*, Madison, Wisconsin, November 1998, and in *Himal*, Katmandu, Nepal, March 1999.

The interview for chapter 1 took place at Hampshire College in Amherst, Massachusetts, on December 14–15, 1996; the interview for chapter 2 took place at Hampshire College on August 24, 1998; and the interview for chapter 3 took place in Boulder, Colorado, on October 12–13, 1998.

صبحِ آزادی

(اگست ۱۹۴۷ء)

یہ داغ داغ اُجالا، یہ شب گزیدہ سحر
وہ انتظار تھا جس کا، یہ وہ سحر تو نہیں
یہ وہ سحر تو نہیں جس کی آرزو لے کر
چلے تھے یار کہ مل جائے گی کہیں نہ کہیں

فلک کے دشت میں تاروں کی آخری منزل
کہیں تو ہوگا شبِ سست موج کا ساحل
کہیں تو جا کے رکے گا سفینۂ غمِ دل

جوان لہو کی پُراسرار شاہراہوں سے
چلے جو یار تو دامن پہ کتنے ہاتھ پڑے
دیارِ حُسن کی بے صبر خواب گاہوں سے
پکارتی رہیں باہیں، بدن بلاتے رہے

بہت عزیز تھی لیکن رخِ سحر کی لگن
بہت قریں تھا حسیناں نور کا دامن
سبک سبک تھی تمنا، دبی دبی تھی تھکن

سنا ہے ہو بھی چکا ہے فراقِ ظلمت و نور
سنا ہے ہو بھی چکا ہے وصالِ منزل و گام
بدل چکا ہے بہت اہلِ درد کا دستور
نشاطِ وصل حلال و عذابِ ہجر حرام

جگر کی آگ، نظر کی اُمنگ، دل کی جلن
کسی پہ چارۂ ہجراں کا کچھ اثر ہی نہیں
کہاں سے آئی نگارِ صبا، کدھر کو گئی
ابھی چراغِ سرِ رہ کو کچھ خبر ہی نہیں

ابھی گرانیِ شب میں کمی نہیں آئی
نجاتِ دیدہ و دل کی گھڑی نہیں آئی
چلے چلو کہ وہ منزل ابھی نہیں آئی

فیضؔ

DAWN OF FREEDOM (AUGUST 1947)

These tarnished rays, this night-smudged light—
This is not that Dawn for which, ravished with freedom,
we had set out in sheer longing,
so sure that somewhere in its desert the sky harbored
a final haven for the stars, and we would find it.
We had no doubt that night's vagrant wave would stray towards the
    shore,
that the heart rocked with sorrow would at last reach its port.

Friends, our blood shaped its own mysterious roads.
When hands tugged at our sleeves, enticing us to stay,
and from wondrous chambers Sirens cried out
with their beguiling arms, with their bare bodies,
our eyes remained fixed on that beckoning Dawn,
forever vivid in her muslins of transparent light.
Our blood was young—what could hold us back?

Now listen to the terrible rampant lie:
Light has forever been severed from the Dark;
our feet, it is heard, are now one with their goal.
See our leaders polish their manner clean of our suffering:
Indeed, we must confess only to bliss;
we must surrender any utterance for the Beloved—all yearning is
    outlawed.

But the heart, the eye, the yet deeper heart—
Still ablaze for the Beloved, their turmoil shines.
In the lantern by the road the flame is stalled for news:
Did the morning breeze ever come? Where has it gone?
Night weighs us down, it still weighs us down.
Friends, come away from this false light. Come, we must search for that
    promised Dawn.

—*Faiz Ahmed Faiz*
translated from the Urdu by Agha Shahid Ali

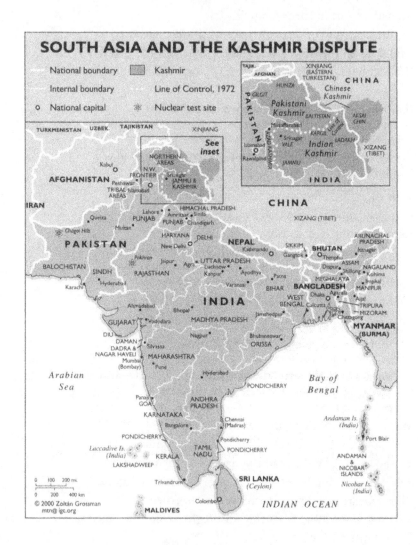

SOUTH ASIA AND THE KASHMIR DISPUTE

National boundary

Internal boundary

○ National capital

Kashmir

Line of Control, 1972

❄ Nuclear test site

EQBAL AHMAD

A BIOGRAPHICAL SKETCH

Eqbal Ahmad was born in the village of Irki in Bihar, India, in 1933 or 1934. A few years later, his father was murdered over a land dispute, while the young Eqbal lay beside him. During the Partition of India in 1947, he and his elder brothers migrated to Pakistan.[1]

Ahmad graduated from Foreman Christian College in Lahore, Pakistan, in 1951 with a degree in economics. After serving briefly as an army officer, he enrolled at Occidental College in California as a Rotary Fellow in American history in 1957. From 1958 to 1960, he studied political science and Middle Eastern history at Princeton, later earning his Ph.D.

From 1960 to 1963, Ahmad lived in North Africa, working primarily in Algeria, where he joined the National Liberation Front and worked with Frantz Fanon. He was a member of the Algerian delegation to peace talks at Evian.

When he returned to the United States, Ahmad taught at the University of Illinois at Chicago (1964–1965) and Cornell University in the School of Labor Relations (1965–1968). During these years, he became known as "one of the earliest and most vocal opponents of American policies in Vietnam and Cambodia."[2] In 1969, he married the teacher and writer Julie Diamond. From 1968 to 1972, he was a fellow at the Adlai Stevenson Institute in Chicago.

In 1971, Ahmad was indicted with the anti-war Catholic priests, Daniel and Philip Berrigan, along with four other Catholic pacifists, on charges of conspiracy to kidnap Henry Kissinger. After fifty-nine hours of deliberations, the jury declared a mistrial.

From 1972 to 1982, Ahmad was Senior Fellow at the Institute for Policy Studies. From 1973 to 1975, he served as the first director of its overseas affiliate, the Transnational Institute in Amsterdam.

In 1982, Ahmad joined the faculty at Hampshire College in Amherst, Massachusetts, where he taught world politics and political science.

In the early 1990s, he was granted a parcel of land in Pakistan by Prime Minister Benazir Bhutto's government to build an independent, alternative university, named Khaldunia. The land was later seized by Bhutto's husband, Asif Zardari, reportedly to build a golf course and club.[3]

A prolific writer and activist, Ahmad was widely consulted by revolutionaries, journalists, activist leaders, and policymakers around the world. He was an editor of the journal *Race and Class*, contributing editor of *Middle East Report* and *L'Economiste du Tiers Monde*, co-founder of *Pakistan Forum*, and an editorial board member of *Arab Studies Quarterly*. Ahmad was "that rare thing, an intellectual unintimidated by power or authority, a companion in arms to such diverse figures as Noam Chomsky, Howard Zinn, Ibrahim Abu-Lughod, Richard Falk, Fred Jameson, Alexander Cockburn, and Daniel Berrigan."[4]

Upon his retirement from Hampshire in 1997, he settled permanently in Pakistan, where he continued to write a weekly column for *Dawn*, Pakistan's oldest English-language newspaper. Eqbal Ahmad died in Islamabad on May 11, 1999, of heart failure following surgery for colon cancer, diagnosed just one week before.

NOTES

1   Edward W. Said, "He Brought Wisdom and Integrity to the Cause of Oppressed People," *Guardian*, May 14, 1999, p. 22.

2   Michael T. Kaufman, "Eqbal Ahmad: Scholar and Antiwar Activist, Dies at 67," *New York Times*, May 13, 1999, p. C22.

3   Abid Aslam, "Memories of a Hopeful Prankster: Celebrating the Life of Eqbal Ahmad," *Toward Freedom* 48: 4 (August 1999): 23.

4   Said, "He Brought Wisdom and Integrity to the Cause of Oppressed People."

FOREWORD
TO THE SECOND EDITION

BY PERVEZ HOODBHOY

Confronting Empire is aptly titled. At a time when the world order created by the United States after World War II is unraveling, China is rising, and U.S. strength is on the wane, there are calls to make America great again. One can easily forget that this nostalgia is for the decades when the United States was an aggressive, bellicose power. Between 1945 and 1995 it had fought twenty-three major wars as well as countless minor ones. Korea, Guatemala, Congo, Laos, Peru, Vietnam, Cambodia, El Salvador, and Nicaragua are only some of the countries that it had bombed or invaded. The United States had overthrown elected governments, used targeted killing, napalm, chemical defoliants, and cluster munitions, and built a nuclear arsenal able to end the world. Surely this empire needed and needs to be confronted.

I see it now, but confrontation was the last thought I had in mind when in 1969 I got off the plane from Pakistan as a nineteen-year-old heading to MIT to be a first-year student. This was a time when things were stirring in the imperial heartland against yet another war, this one in Vietnam. Even at MIT—a key bastion of technology that powered the postwar American empire—the protests had assumed force. But, as a techie type from an elite Pakistani high school where students are typically thoughtless and career obsessed, I was neither aware of nor cared about larger issues.

The first time I actually saw Eqbal Ahmad was when he spoke at an anti-war rally outside the MIT Student Center sometime in 1970 where he was sharing the platform with Noam Chomsky, Salvador Luria, and

Howard Zinn. It started out with me being a curious onlooker, but it was the beginning of a profound transformation. Eqbal's oratory had left me stunned, releasing a strange energy within me. Then, some weeks later, at my invitation, he returned to speak about the genocide in East Pakistan.

Back in those days only the tiniest minority of West Pakistanis in the United States, including both students and those settled there, had any sympathy with the Bengalis who were now being massacred by the tens of thousands. In fact, the majority of us West Pakistanis wanted a still harsher response to their agitation for a separate state. In these adverse circumstances Eqbal Ahmad, together with Feroz Ahmad and Aijaz Ahmad (no relation to each other), had started a frankly traitorous magazine called *Pakistan Progressive* that sought to rally Pakistanis in North America against their army's actions. I became the magazine's campus promoter and distributor.

Eqbal championed causes of those oppressed and dispossessed. It didn't matter where: Algeria, Vietnam, Pakistan, and Palestine. In his foreword here, his friend Edward Said speaks to Eqbal's "heroic defense, his unstinting sense of solidarity with, my people, the Palestinians. For many refugees, camp dwellers, and wretched of the earth who have been forgotten by their fellow Arabs and Muslims, Eqbal was one of their guiding lights." Ostracized by most of the American academic community for his passionate advocacy of Palestinian rights, Eqbal had remained an itinerant professor at several U.S. universities for much of his life. He recalled that his colleagues at Cornell chose to stand elsewhere rather than sit with him at the same cafeteria table.

With a strong memory for events and people, an uncanny ability to quickly grasp the essence of a political situation, and a large circle of contacts that kept him informed, Eqbal achieved a reputation for being prescient. He had warned Yasir Arafat that firing Katyusha rockets from South Lebanon into Israel would achieve nothing beyond brutal Israeli retaliation. Indeed, it came just as he had predicted. As Beirut was destroyed block after block, Eqbal was burning from within, helpless and frustrated by his inability to prevent the carnage. This emotional state probably had something to do with the fact that he suffered his first heart attack in 1982.

It was natural that I started seeing the world through Eqbal's eyes. I remember it was late evening in Islamabad—morning time in New York—when I entered the living room of my house on the campus of

Quaid-e-Azam University. The first airliner had already crashed into the World Trade Center. Aghast, my wife and I watched the second plane strike, shoots of fire emerge, and the towers collapse in slow motion. No, she said, it wasn't an animation or a video game. My first thought—the world would now see hell. My second strayed to Eqbal: who would he have said had done it? What was likely to happen next? And, might we have again quarreled on the causes and responsibility?

It had already been two-and-a-half years since Eqbal had passed away, leaving us all with a grief that just would not go away. As I write this seventeen years later, my eyes blur. That's unusual even though I eventually became part of his family—his niece, Hajra Ahmad, and I had married twenty-five years before his death—and he dearly loved our children. But that still doesn't explain it because I am just one of so many who knew him—and there were hundreds across the world—who also had this sense of infinite loss.

So what is it that drew people instinctively toward this man? I have no clear answer. Perhaps it was because you felt he deeply cared about you. It wasn't faked; he somehow had a capacity to hold so much and give so much. He was an attentive listener who somehow made time for individual stories; few in this fast-paced world have patience for this. If you had a problem, you went to him, and you would come back feeling less burdened.

Eqbal passed away in 1999. Today, almost two decades later, no issue burns more fiercely than that of Islam in the contemporary world. His vision and voice would have been a key part of the global conversation if he had lived. A life-long involvement with Algeria, Palestine, Kashmir, Pakistan, and India led Eqbal to a firm position on many Muslim causes as well as a profound understanding of Islam's relationship to power and politics. He saw Muslims as wretched and dispossessed, betrayed by their leaders, the hapless victims of a predatory imperial system. With his Muslim roots he felt a deep empathy for the Muslim predicament while, at the same time, maintaining a strictly secular outlook on life. Even as his life ebbed away, I did not see him make any supplications or any attempt to pray. So let me try to present Eqbal's position on Muslims and Islam in the modern world. I will try to do it as fairly as I can. I must admit, however, that I cannot agree with it in totality.

The future of Muslim societies can only lie, Eqbal believed, in allowing Islamic values of justice, equality, and tolerance to shape power and politics but without the formalistic imposition of structures and strictures of centuries past. For him it was values, knowledge, aesthetics, and style that had defined Islamic civilization and invested it with greatness. But "don't hanker for the past" was his message. Those who glorify the past and seek to re-create it, almost invariably fail, while those who view it comprehensively and critically are able to draw on the past in meaningful and lasting ways. "The admiration for Emperor Aurangzeb is a symptom of a deep ailment," he wrote, adding that that in Pakistan, Islam has been a convenient refuge of troubled and weak leaders. Reacting against Pakistani prime minister Nawaz Sharif's call in 1998 for an Islamic state governed by sharia principles, he ascribed it to "a protracted crisis of leadership" and an attempt to distract attention away from core issues.

Political-religious movements that purport to create an Islamic state, and which have adopted terror as their weapon, have done enormous damage to Muslims, said Eqbal. They wage holy wars and commit atrocities sanctimoniously, yet nothing is truly sacred to them. They spill blood in bazaars, in homes and in courts, mosques, and churches. They believe themselves to be God's warriors, above man-made laws and the judgment of mankind. In doing so, they surrender the most potent weapon of the weak—the moral high ground. For Eqbal, Mahatma Gandhi and nonviolence had a lesson for us all.

What explains the rise of extremist political-religious movements? Certainly, "Islamic fundamentalism" is a common enough epithet used by the Western media for the Muslim variety. But, Eqbal insisted, neither Muslims nor Jews nor Hindus are unique in this respect. All variants of contemporary fundamentalism, he said, reduce complex religious systems and civilizations to one or another version of modern fascism. They are concerned with power, not with the soul, and they mobilize people for political purposes rather than with the goal of sharing or alleviating their sufferings and aspirations. All brands of religious fundamentalisms are reflections of a common problem, with shared roots and similar patterns of expression.

These shared roots, said Eqbal, lie in global changes that are occurring much too fast for successful human adaptation. For millennia, humanity had experienced the unsettling process of change. But the global transformation made possible by technology and communication is so systemic that it destroys the autonomy of life lived for millennia, forcing diverse peoples and individuals to live in urban proximity and compete with each other. Caught in this furious tempest of modernity and change, cultures do adapt, but relatively slowly and often painfully. How peacefully and democratically a society makes this journey depends on its historical circumstances. But activists need not be fatalistic and leave social change to the blind forces of technology and economics. What matters equally is "the engagement of its intelligentsia, the outlook of its leaders and governments, and the ideological choices they make."

Death has interrupted our conversation, one that I would have much wanted to pursue further. I cannot claim to have definite answers to the questions we debated nor know the way ahead. Can Muslims be weaned away from the notion that they are superior to everyone else and, by virtue of possessing the perfect book, have also inherited the master plan for a utopia on earth as well as the rewards in the afterlife? Post–bin Laden, but in the age of Abu Bakr Al-Baghdadi and Boko Haram, what is the alternative to high-tech weapons, clear-cut military doctrines, and the relentless deployment of military force?

Eqbal's answers would have drawn on his commitment to being a staunch humanist and activist fighting for the voiceless and the oppressed. He cared deeply and was willing to believe people could endure and be more brave and creative than they knew. He saw the big picture and still knew the value of individual stories. His incisive and lucid way of thinking and his voice are clear and sharp in these skillful interviews with David Barsamian.

August 2016

INTRODUCTION

BY DAVID BARSAMIAN

It is difficult to think of Eqbal Ahmad in the past tense. As I look at his words, I hear his lilting accent and mellifluous voice ringing in my ears. Eqbal was very fond of Urdu poetry and used it as a tool of analysis. One of its main motifs is paradox. So, I write with a mixture of joy and sadness. Joy that we have this book and sadness that Eqbal is not with us.

I remember the gleam in Eqbal's eye and his enthusiastic response when I first proposed doing a series of interviews for a book. The idea had great appeal to him. He had written the introduction to *The Pen and The Sword*, my book with Edward Said.[1] And he was familiar with my work with Noam Chomsky and Howard Zinn.[2] More than that, we met in a curious way, albeit he was older, on the same "kinare" or riverbank. I always felt a connection with Eqbal. I had spent some time in South Asia and spoke his language, Urdu, and shared his appreciation of and admiration for Indo-Islamic culture. Although I had not been displaced myself, my parents had been—and the upheaval and turmoil they went through marked me deeply.

I knew of Eqbal and his activism long before we actually met. Our first interview in 1983 in New York was memorable and instructive. We sat at his kitchen table and talked about the third world, imperialism, and dependency. I thought, "I've got a great interview" and couldn't wait to hear the results. As soon as I came home, I turned the tape recorder on only to discover that the tape was blank! Alas, I had failed to press the record button. As they say in South Asia, "What to do, *baba*?" With trepidation and embarrassment, I called Eqbal and told him of my gaffe. He said, "No problem. Come over and we'll do it again." And, indeed, a day or two later we re-did the interview. Generosity and graciousness marked the man. Over the years, whenever I told the story, his friends would nod and say, "That's Eqbal."

Our interview time passed quickly and almost effortlessly, even though they lasted as long as six hours. He had an easy conversational style that was at once compelling and inviting. Our discussions were punctuated by spicy food and glasses of wine. During a break from one marathon session in August 1998, we took a walk around Mt. Holyoke. He was in a pensive and reflective mood. It was then he told me that his health was not so good. Ten months later, he was dead.

The topics covered in these interviews are as current as when we first discussed them: economic decay and breathtaking misrule in Pakistan (a country again under military control since General Pervez Musharraf ousted Nawaz Sharif in October 1999), Hindu fundamentalism, nuclear weapons in South Asia, Kashmir, Afghanistan, the Balkans, Sri Lanka, sectarianism, pathologies of power, the implosion of third-world countries, and the overarching issue of U.S. imperialism. While others backed off from using the term, Eqbal never hesitated. His good friend Pervez Hoodbhoy commented after hearing Eqbal lecture for the first time that he had never heard "such a devastating combination of knowledge, eloquence, and passion used with unerring precision to shatter the myths and lies that surrounded America's imperial adventure."

There is a lot of claptrap these days about public intellectuals. Eqbal Ahmad was a rare combination of scholar and activist. He not only shared his knowledge with progressive movements for social change but he participated in them. He cared about people and he cared about justice.

The second interview ends with a Muhammad Iqbal couplet which expresses a sentiment that echoes in these pages. Eqbal Ahmad was "someone capable of seeing inside."

Boulder, Colorado
May 2000

NOTES

1   Eqbal Ahmad, "Introduction," in Edward W. Said, *The Pen and the Sword: Conversations with David Barsamian* (Monroe, Maine: Common Courage Press, 1994).

2   See Howard Zinn, *The Future of History: Conversations with David Barsamian* (Monroe, Maine: Common Courage Press, 1999), and Noam Chomsky, *The Common Good: Noam Chomsky Interviewed by David Barsamian* (Monroe, Maine: Common Courage Press/Odonian Press Real Stories Series, 1998).

CHERISH THE MAN'S COURAGE

BY EDWARD W. SAID

Despite the many hours of praise and celebration deservedly heaped on our dear friend and comrade Eqbal Ahmad, there's still a great deal more to be said about him. I flatter myself that I can at least try to say more. One of the most remarkable things about him was that even though he crossed more borders and traversed more boundaries than most people, Eqbal was reassuringly himself in each new place, new situation, new context. This was not at all a matter of ethnic or religious identity, nor did it have much to do with the habitual stability we associate with solid citizens. Rather, Eqbal's special blend of intellectual brilliance and courage, supernally accurate analysis, and consistently humane and warm presence made of him, to paraphrase from Rudyard Kipling's *Kim*, a friend of the whole world.[1]

In recalling the many different places and times in which I met Eqbal, from Chicago to Beirut to New York to Tunisia to Amherst and elsewhere, I find myself marveling at how easily he became a new person acting in a totally new situation and yet preserved these fundamental characteristics which stamped him for all time as a true friend and comrade. Eqbal always has time for students, young people, friends, people in need, partners in struggle. No one I'd ever known was as prodigally generous with his time, his knowledge, his goods, as he. In all the years I knew him, he never turned me down by saying that he was too busy or too tied up with something else. I made far too many demands on him, but he was always ready to listen, ready to help analyze a problem, a difficult situation, the embarrassments or terrors of some political or personal quandary.

Let me give one example of the trust that he inspired and the care that he took with his friends. In 1987, a group of highly influential rabbinical figures who were well known in their support for Israel wanted to have a private discussion with me. I gathered that they, too, were puzzled about Palestinian intentions, and more profoundly about the persistence of a Palestinian resistance to Israeli practices. Significantly enough, our meeting was to take place a few months before the beginning of the *intifada*. I had already been fairly involved in off-the-record and in some cases secret meetings with Israeli and American Jewish leaders and was uncertain as to how to proceed, since all our other meetings were both inconclusive and often futile, so great was the gap between us, as relatively independent Palestinians without much organizational power or support, and the much more estimable, well-established Jewish members, with their dozens of organizations, privileged relationships with Israel, and so on.

I had already by that time established Eqbal as my guru on matters political. So the first thing I did was ask him whether I should have that meeting. He said yes. I asked him immediately to come with me. In this case, as in all others, he agreed. Although neither a Palestinian nor a participant in the previous meetings I've described, Eqbal had immediately stood out as the one person I could totally trust to be there, to tell the truth, to help guide me, and to provide an additional credible voice. Throughout the meeting, Eqbal was extraordinarily poised and calm as he negotiated the challenges and provocations of what were for me pitfalls and traps into which I kept falling. When at one point in the three-hour discussion one of the Jewish leaders said that even though he had made lots of speeches calling Yasir Arafat a terrorist and a Hitler, he, this leader, knew that he wasn't telling the truth, Eqbal quietly and deliberately pointed out to him what unnecessary hypocrisy he had indulged himself in, something I could not say myself.

One more story is worth recounting. In the late 1970s, I was able to invite Eqbal to Beirut, where he met Arafat and other Palestinian leaders, who immediately recognized his skill and sincerity of analysis. It was in the summer of 1980, during the Lebanese civil war, that Eqbal prevailed on Abu Jihad, Arafat's colleague and the PLO's military commander in south Lebanon and elsewhere, to let him go on a tour of PLO positions in south Lebanon. Eqbal did so and a few days later produced a detailed report for them about his findings. In essence, Eqbal not only predicted the fact of the Israeli invasion that was to take place two years thence, in 1982, but was also able, alas, to predict the result.

It wasn't only his skill in military matters that was impressive. Those leaders sensed about Eqbal that he was a real friend in the struggle and his sincerity and commitment could not be gainsaid, despite the fact that he wasn't a native. True, he knew how to exploit his own Asian and non-white provenance. I don't say this at all critically, but rather admiringly. And in the case of the Palestinians they knew they were dealing with a fellow Muslim. But anyone who knew Eqbal in conditions of struggle knew subliminally that his loyalty and solidarity were unquestionable. He was a genius at sympathy. When he used the pronoun "we," you knew that he spoke and acted as one of us, but never at the expense either of his honesty or of his critical faculties, which reigned supreme. This is why Eqbal came as close to being a really free man as anyone can be.

This isn't to say that he was indifferent to the problems of others, or blessed in that he didn't have problems of his own. This was very far from true. But he did give one the impression that he was always his own man, always able to think and act clearly for himself and, if asked, for others. His subcontinental origins in Bihar and Lahore steeped him both in the travails of empire and in the many wasteful tragedies of decolonization, of which sectarian hatred and violence, plus separatism and partition, are among the worst.

Yet retrospective bitterness at what the white man wrought and at what his fellow Indians and Pakistanis did were never part of Eqbal's response. He was always more interested in creativity than in vindictiveness, in originality of spirit and method than in mere radicalism, in generosity and complexity of analysis over the tight neatness of his fellow political scientists. The title of one of his most spirited essays, on Régis Debray, was entitled "Radical but Wrong."[2]

When I dedicated my book *Culture and Imperialism* to him, it was because in his activity, life, and thinking Eqbal embodied not just the politics of empire but that whole fabric of experience expressed in human life itself, rather than in economic rules and reductive formulas.[3] What Eqbal understood about the experience of empire was the domination of empire in all its forms, but also the creativity, originality, and vision created in resistance to it. Those words—"creativity," "originality," "vision"—were central to his attitudes on politics and history.

Among Eqbal's earliest writings on Vietnam was a series of papers on revolutionary warfare which was intended as a refutation of standard American doctrine on the subject. U.S. counterinsurgency experts see in Vietnamese resistance a sort of conspiratorial, technically adept, communist and terrorist uprising, which can be defeated with superior weapons, clear-cut pragmatic doctrines, and the relentless deployment of overwhelming military force. What Eqbal suggested was a different paradigm: the revolutionary guerrilla as someone with a real commitment to justice who has the support of her or his people, and who is willing to sacrifice for the sake of a cause or ideology that has mobilized people. What counterinsurgency doctrine cannot admit is that the native elites whose interests are congruent not with their country's but with those of the United States are not the people to win a revolutionary war. In confronting the arch-theorist of this benighted view—none other than Samuel Huntington—Eqbal put it this way:

> In underdeveloped countries the quiescence which followed independence is giving way to new disappointments and new demands which are unlikely to be satisfied by a politics of boundary management and selective cooptation—a fact which the United States, much like our ruling elites, is yet unable or unwilling to perceive. There is an increasingly perceptible gap between our need for social transformation and America's insistence on stability, between our impatience for change and America's obsession with order, our move toward revolution and America's belief in the plausibility of achieving reforms under the robber barons of the "third world," our longing for absolute national sovereignty and America's preference for pliable allies, our desire to see our national soil freed of foreign occupation and America's alleged need for military bases. . . . As the gap widens between our sorrow and America's contentment, so will, perhaps, these dichotomies of our perspectives and our priorities. Unless there is a fundamental redefinition of American interests and goals, our confrontations with the United States will be increasingly antagonistic. In the client states of Asia and Latin America it may even be tragic. In this sense Vietnam may not be so unique. It may be a warning of things to come.[4]

What emerges in these writings is the opposition between conventional and unconventional thought and of course the even deeper opposition between justice and injustice. In his preference for what the unconventional and the just can bring peoples by way of liberation, invigorated culture, and well-being, Eqbal was firm and uncompromising. His distrust for standing armies, frozen bureaucracies, persistent oligarchies allowed no exceptions. Yet at the same time, as he showed in his great essay on Debray, it is not enough to be unconventional if that means having no regard for tradition, for the goods that women and men enjoy, for the great stabilities of human life. Eqbal was shrewd and illusionless enough to realize that overturning societies for the sake of revolution only, without sufficient attention to the fact that human beings also love and create and celebrate and commemorate, is a callous, merely destructive practice that may be radical but is profoundly wrong.

After allowing Debray to celebrate rather romantically the virtues of being a guerrilla in the mountains, Eqbal provided this Burkian note, a corrective for the callow exuberance of someone who had not thought long and hard enough about the realities of human political and social life: "[P]ersonal virtues and even group experiences do not easily transfer to national and public institutions."[5] Worst yet, there is the startling paradox that Debray's insufficient vision translates perfectly into its opposite, American counterinsurgency doctrine, personified by, among others, Walt Whitman Rostow. Thus, far from being a true revolution, that is, a popular movement that goes the whole way from uprising to democratic institutions, Debray's theory lends itself to ephemeral results rather than to lasting positive effects in the real world in which men and women have to live. Yet even though Eqbal criticized Debray quite severely, he saw in the man's work, with typical generosity, a "timeless appeal."[6]

Most of Eqbal's writing was in some way not only inflected or directly influenced by his Indian and Pakistani experiences, but also by his Algerian experience. His elusiveness about dates and his reluctance to spend too much time talking about his own exploits have led me to conclude this period was absolutely central to all his work. There is first of all the importance of a human factor and the necessity of out-organizing the enemy rather than simply out-fighting him. There is second the need to de-legitimize the colonial or unjust authority and create parallel organizations to help the people live away from the usurpers' power. Then last, and perhaps most important, there is the need to transmute the structures of war into democratic and national institutions. Eqbal's article about Algeria recorded the successes of the first two factors and the failure of the third.[7] Hence, he wrote, with the monopoly of power gathered first by Algerian President Ahmed ben Bella and then by President Houari Boumedienne after him, the National Liberation Front atrophied into the sullen, murderous bureaucracy now involved in the horrific bloodbath of present-day Algeria. But despite this massive failure, Eqbal did not devalue the triumph of revolutionary victory or lose hope in the possibility of true liberation. Here the influence of Frantz Fanon, his comrade, is implicit. We didn't drive out, Fanon said, the white policemen to fill their places with black or brown policemen. Out of national consciousness must come a new social consciousness, a test which for the most part the post-colonial countries have failed.[8]

No one has more trenchantly summarized the various pathologies of power in the third world than Eqbal in the three summary essays he wrote for *Arab Studies Quarterly* in 1980 and 1981.[9] Once again, unlike many of the second-thoughters and post-Marxists who populate the academic and liberal journals today, Eqbal remained true to the ideals of revolution and truer yet to its unfulfilled promise. To have heard him lecture over the years, passionately and sternly, about militarism in the Arab world, in Pakistan, in Algeria and elsewhere, was to have known the high moral position he took on matters having to do with the sanctity and potential dignity of human life either squandered or abused by strutting dictators or co-opted intellectuals. Creativity, vision, and originality of the kind appreciated by Eqbal in his great friend the Urdu poet Faiz Ahmed Faiz are the measure for political life, not the trappings of honor guards, fancy limousines, and enormously bloated and all-powerful bureaucracies. The measure is the human being, not the abstract law or the amoral power.

I think it must have been difficult to hold on to such ideals and principles. Most of Eqbal's written work, and indeed his activism, took place in dark times. Not only did he take full stock of the devastations of imperialism and injustice all over the globe, but in particular he more eloquently than anyone else inventoried the particular sadness and low points reached by Islamic cultures and states. Yet even then he managed to remind us that what he mourned is no mere religious or cultural fanaticism, as it is usually misrepresented in the West, but a widespread ecumenical movement. Moreover, though not an Arab himself, Eqbal reminded Arabs that Arabism, far from being a narrow-based nationalism, is quite unique in the history of nationalisms because it tried to connect itself beyond boundaries. It came close to imagining a universal community linked by word and sentiment alone. Anyone who is an Arab in his feelings, in his language and his culture, is an Arab. So a Jew is an Arab. A Christian is an Arab. A Muslim is an Arab. A Kurd is an Arab. I know of no national movement which defined itself so broadly.

In such a situation and with such a heritage, Eqbal saw the degradation of ideas and values that grip Arabs and Muslims alike. Let me quote him again. This is in the aftermath of the Gulf War in 1993:

> We live in scoundrel times. This is the dark age of Muslim history, the age of surrender and collaboration, punctuated by madness. The decline of our civilization began in the eighteenth century when, in the intellectual embrace of orthodoxy, we skipped the age of enlightenment and the scientific revolution. In the second half of the twentieth century, it has fallen.
>
> I have been a lifelong witness to surrender, and imagined so many times—as a boy in 1948, a young man in 1967 . . . and approaching middle age in 1982—that finally we have hit rock bottom, that the next time even if we go down we would manage to do so with a modicum of dignity. Fortunately, I did not entertain even so modest an illusion from Saddam Hussein's loudly proclaimed "mother of battles."[10]

This on the one hand and on the other the multiple degradations of what he once called the fascism and separatism, two clearly identifiable, seemingly hostile but symbiotically linked trends, in his Pakistan. Former Pakistani prime minister Zulfikar Ali Bhutto and his family, former president General Muhammad Zia ul-Haq, and their coteries plundered the land, demoralized the population. They tried to subdue the country's insurrectionary constituent cultures and failed, but at the price of more blood and treasure. And everywhere, as throughout the Muslim world, they provoked, if they did not actually cause, the rise of Islamism, which as a secularist Eqbal always deplored.

But ever the fighter and activist, he did not submit in resignation. He wrote more and more in earnest and in 1994 undertook his grand project of founding a new university in Pakistan—Khaldunia, aptly named after the great Arab historian and founder of sociology, Ibn Khaldun. In this project and his enthusiasm for it, Eqbal was no Don Quixote, tilting at windmills, but like Marxist theoretician Antonio Gramsci, he took as his motto "Pessimism of the intellect, optimism of the will."[11] This was part of the man's rareness, knowing how to rescue the best available in a tradition without illusion or melodramatic self-dramatization. For him, Islam, Arabism, and American idealism were treasures to be tapped, despite tyrants like Zia ul-Haq and Henry Kissinger, whose manipulations and cold-blooded policies debase and bring down everything they touch.

Something about Eqbal that touched and helped me more deeply than almost anything he did or wrote was his heroic defense, his unstinting sense of solidarity with, my people, the Palestinians. For the many refugees, camp dwellers, and wretched of the earth who have been forgotten by their own leaders and their fellow Arabs and Muslims, Eqbal was one of their guiding lights. And for that, no Palestinian can ever thank him enough. I saw him with our young people, with our leaders, with professionals, intellectuals, children, and old people. There was never anything but affection and sympathy from him for them. All of them, and I could see it in their eyes, cherished the man's courage, brilliance, and sheer downright humaneness. But what also needs mentioning is that to struggle for Palestine as Eqbal did was to have none of the material or even intellectual rewards of the struggle. Palestine is a thankless cause, one in which if you truly serve you get nothing back but opprobrium, abuse, and ostracism. Eqbal suffered all these. His outspoken, uncompromising solidarity with us cost him dearly, not only in hours and days and months of wasted effort; not only in the disappointments, the deaths and disfigurements, that have distorted our lives, perhaps irremediably; not only in the endless surrenders and humiliations, the failures of reason and planning, but also—and this must be emphasized, since Eqbal himself would never say it—in the cost to him, in his profession, in his career, maybe even in his writing. Palestine is the cruelest, most difficult cause to uphold, not because it is unjust, but because it is just and yet dangerous to speak about as honestly and as concretely as Eqbal did.

How many friends avoid the subject? How many colleagues want none of Palestine's controversy? How many *bien pensant* liberals have time for Bosnia and Chechnya and Somalia and Rwanda and South Africa and Nicaragua and Vietnam and human and civil rights everywhere on earth, but not for Palestine and Palestinians? Not Eqbal, though, to the embarrassment and shame of so many of his friends. He spoke, wrote, and constantly brought the matter up, like a child who refused to be cowed by adults and managed to blurt out the nasty family secret that everyone was trying to hide from. For all this, I and so many of us are grateful and will never forget what Eqbal said and did. The beauty of it was that he has not been merely an unruly cheerleader or an uncritical enthusiast, but a sober, even somber, critic of our struggle for self-determination; never merely negative, but always ready with positive, sometimes ingenious and visionary suggestions (none of which, alas, were ever taken up, to our eternal discredit).

I was always impressed and often stunned by the delicacy and sensitivity of Eqbal's attitudes toward Israeli Jews. During that encounter with Jewish leaders in 1987, he lectured them on the fact that we were dealing with, as he put it, "two communities of suffering." So catholic and unrestrained were his capacities for understanding the travails of all peoples that he never descended either into conspiracy theories or downright anti-Semitism. On the contrary, there was always a kind of grave nobility to what he had to say to and about Israeli Jews. And he always conveyed that special scrupulosity of attention to non-Israeli Jews, who might otherwise have bristled at the severity of his anti-Israeli critique.

In the 1970s, he formulated the suggestion, an extremely brilliant one, quite in keeping with his general attitude of non-violent aggressiveness, that the PLO should try to organize a march of Palestinians toward the Israeli borders in Jordan, Lebanon, and Syria. Inspired by the great civil rights marches of the 1960s, Eqbal urged Arafat and company to mobilize as many people as possible, walking unarmed to the borders, with banners saying, "We want to go home." I remember the look on their faces, when I patiently explained Eqbal's proposal, of disbelief and mild panic, especially when I emphasized the need for peaceful means and disciplined organization. This was at a time when Eqbal was mercilessly critical of the cult of the gun, the misuse of slogans like "armed struggle," and the creeping, ultimately debilitating militarism of Palestinian thinking and organization. At a seminar convened in Beirut for Eqbal, he painstakingly propounded a strategy for mounting an organized campaign for Palestinian human rights in the United States. He explained that we needed detailed information on every congressional district in the United States, on the workings of important civil institutions such as the churches, colleges, and labor unions, all of which could have been done with one-tenth of the resources that were squandered on first-class air tickets, an expanding bureaucracy, and bottles and bottles of Black

Label whiskey. Ten years later, he repeated a similar but more detailed argument to the exiled Palestinian leadership in Tunis with, I'm sorry to say, the same results. Arafat later told me, "You and Eqbal have constantly been telling us that we should try to understand America. Well, I've appointed an America committee at the highest levels of the PLO. It will do the most advanced research, give us all the options, and so on. I hope you realize how the two of you have succeeded."

A year after that, I discovered that the committee had indeed been appointed and, as if it was something straight out of *Gulliver's Travels*, was composed entirely of people who knew no English. They never met, and they managed to appoint only one full-time researcher, a very bright woman, who told me that "research" meant that she had persuaded her superiors to allow her to buy a subscription to *Time* magazine and occasionally to buy the *International Herald Tribune*. So much for a vigilant and alert leadership.

I think Eqbal and I both knew at the time, although I don't recall that we spoke about it, that something else was afoot that had nothing to do with a grassroots movement. It had to do with looking for a deal with the Americans that would keep Arafat and his followers in power, albeit as collaborators of the Israeli occupation. Eqbal was one of the few prophetic voices raised in criticism of the Oslo accords, which he called "a peace of the weak," while Arafat was constantly referring to it—embarrassing me, I'm sorry to say—as the "peace of the braves," as if he were talking about the baseball team.[12] Never content merely to curse the darkness, Eqbal spoke to me in 1996, at the time of the tunnel incident in Jerusalem's old city, about what, given his unenviable position, Arafat might do. A few days later, I wrote about Eqbal's proposal in one of my regular columns in the Arabic press.[13] By that time, Eqbal and I had become journalists in the local media. We both felt the need to address our own people and stop worrying about how we could get something published in the appalling *New York Times*.

Eqbal proposed that rather than squander the moral legitimacy of Arafat's anti-settlement drive on fruitless street battles that would only lose him more women and men, which is in fact what happened, Arafat should lead a march to one of the settlements, saying, "We are unarmed. We do not want to fight you. But we are going to fight your bricks and your stones." Instead, Arafat sat in one of his bunkers and ordered a general strike that only hurt the Palestinians whose shops were forced shut, and more businesses were lost.

Eqbal brilliantly summarized the current situation with accuracy and with the innate fairness and definitiveness that were the hallmarks of his writing. The Israeli government is now planning roads, major highways and communication networks which link the settlements to the Israeli cities and ports and leave the Palestinian communities out. So we have these autonomous zones which are to be administered by the Palestinian Authority, over which this Authority has no sovereignty. It can't control the land. It can't protect the water. It can't even set up industries without Israel's permission. So we have a series of bantustans called Autonomous Palestinian Authority. Israel is absolving itself of responsibility for the occupied population while keeping the occupation.

It's a brilliant scheme, and it is so far succeeding. Arafat is a party to this tragedy. What we are witnessing is the institutionalization of a system of exclusion, a fully contracted apartheid: separate municipalities, separate schools, separate health systems, a native economy and an indigenous substratum on the margins of the Israeli state beneath the privileged settler society.

This is a bad dream, a racialist utopia being constructed, ironically, by one of the most enlightened and historically humane people, and this with the agreement of a secular native leadership. If the trend holds, during the next decade, Israel-Palestine shall look very much like what has just past, South Africa of the apartheid era.

The range of Eqbal's work as an activist, intellectual, scholar, teacher, and friend was vast. Like very few others, he traversed oceans and boundaries with skill and an enviable sense of familiarity, never intimidated by expertise or professionalized jargon. He honed his language into a marvelously lean instrument in which abstractions came to life and the concrete human experience of people all over the earth was rendered with liveliness and precision. Following is an extract from his introduction, titled "Portent of a New Century," to *Beyond the Storm: A Gulf Crisis Reader*. Note the remarkably fine deployment of generalization, the consistent sense of irony, the regulated anger of his prose; and note also the way his sentences neither maunder nor cringe from harsh truths and how each one contains *aperçus* that could be the subject of whole books by pompous authorities such as Samuel Huntington or Zbigniew Brzezinski.

The twentieth has been a century most remarkable for its simultaneous capacity to promise hope and deliver disappointments. And as the end approaches, it seems to me that the century's ending in the same way in which it began: renewed hopes of a just and peaceable world order are being overwhelmed by politicians and warriors whose political minds remain rooted in the past.

For 300 years before the twentieth century dawned, the world had been transforming, a transformation brought about by modern science, technology, and imperialism. It was through this age of capitalist and European expansion that a world system came to be dominated by the West and the international market came to be controlled entirely for the West's benefit. This sounds rather benign, as though the free market was really free and worked merely to the advantage of the fittest. Far from it; Western domination was achieved by force so widespread, institutionalized, and legitimized by religion and morality that to date the epistemology of this universal violence still shapes relations between the Western and non-Western worlds.[14]

As you read this, you feel that a voice of conviction and hope is addressing you, speaking with you rather than lecturing at or hectoring you. This, too, was the essential Eqbal, a companion, fellow student, relentlessly investigative and inquiring, never dogmatic, except on matters of principle and moral justice. For years I—and I'm sure many of you—regretted that he did not write a big book, until I realized that Eqbal has in fact written a very great deal, scattered, in his typically thoughtless way, all over the globe in articles, scholarly pieces, journalistic interventions, and interviews.

Eqbal could never resist being interviewed, which was why wherever he went he was surrounded by people with tape recorders and notepads, anxious to have a one-on-one with him. Trying to get Eqbal to act like a professional was like trying to plow the sea. It was hopeless. But I was encouraged and of course flattered when in 1997, upon his retirement from Hampshire College, he asked me for advice. "What do you think I should do with my time? How should I divide it, and what should I focus on in my writing?" he asked.

I was certainly incapable of giving him at that moment the sort of useful advice he seemed to be requesting from me. But I thought about it a bit more, and I suggested that he go on doing what only he was able to do so well, but please, for all our sakes, and for those of the young, he should try to remember that in addition to being an oral person—a sort of peregrine Muslim sage, and all of us his *chelas*, or disciples—he shouldn't leave his words scattered to the winds or even recorded on tape, but collected and published in several volumes for everyone to read. Then those who didn't have the privilege of knowing him would know what a truly remarkable, gifted man he was. Because, to paraphrase the words of Wordsworth, writing about Milton, "the world has need of thee."[15]

NOTES

This foreword is based on my address at the tribute given to Eqbal Ahmad at Hampshire College, in Amherst, Massachusetts, on October 4, 1997.

1   Rudyard Kipling, *Kim*, ed. Edward W. Said (New York: Viking Press, 1992).

2   Eqbal Ahmad, "Radical But Wrong," *Monthly Review* 20: 23 (July–August 1968): 70–83.

3   Edward W. Said, *Culture and Imperialism* (New York: Alfred A. Knopf, 1993), p. v.

4   Eqbal Ahmad in dialogue with Samuel P. Huntington et al., in *No More Vietnams? The War and the Future of American Policy*, ed. Richard M. Pfeffer (New York: Harper and Row, 1968), p. 243.

5   Eqbal Ahmad, "Radical But Wrong," p. 81.

6   Eqbal Ahmad, "Radical But Wrong," p. 83.

7   Eqbal Ahmad, "Algeria's Unending Tragedy," *Dawn* 50: 257 (September 20, 1997): 13.

8   See Frantz Fanon, *The Wretched of the Earth*, trans. Constance Farrington (New York: Grove Press, 1968).

9   Eqbal Ahmad, "From Potato Sack to Potato Mash: The Contemporary Crisis of the Third World," *Arab Studies Quarterly* 2: 3 (Summer 1980); "Post-Colonial Systems of Power," *Arab Studies Quarterly* 2: 4 (Fall 1980); "The Neo-Fascist State: Notes on the Pathology of Power in the Third World," *Arab Studies Quarterly* 3: 2 (Spring 1981).

10   Eqbal Ahmad, "The Hundred-Hour War," *Dawn* 50: 76 (March 17, 1991): 11.

11   Antonio Gramsci, *Selections from the Prison Notebooks of Antonio Gramsci*, trans. and ed. Quintin Hoare and Geoffrey N. Smith (New York: International Publishers, 1990), p. 175.

12   Eqbal Ahmad, "After the Peace of the Weak," *AlAhram Weekly* 402 (November 5–11, 1998).

13   See Edward W. Said, *The End of the Peace Process: Oslo and After* (New York: Pantheon, 2000), pp. 108–12.

14   Eqbal Ahmad, "Introduction: Portent of a New Century," *Beyond the Storm: A Gulf Crisis Reader*, ed. Phyllis Bennis and Michel Moushabeck (Brooklyn, New York: Olive Branch Press, 1991), p. 7.

15   William Wordsworth, "[Milton! Thou should'st be living at this hour]" (1802), in *The Poetical Works of William Wordsworth*, vol. 3 (London: Edward Moxon, 1849–1850).

CHAPTER ONE

THINK CRITICALLY AND TAKE RISKS

GANDHI AND PARTITION

One of the critical events of your childhood was the murder of your father.

That played an important role, because apart from leaving a very deep scar on me as a child, unconsciously I must have absorbed certain conclusions about life. One was that class is more important than blood relationship and that property is more dear to people than friendship or loyalties. Because in the murder of my father some relatives themselves were involved. They felt their property rights were threatened by his politics. . . . He was involved with nationalism and gifting lands, thus setting bad examples.

When you look back at that fifty-year period in South Asia, with Mahatma Gandhi, the Quit India movement, and then the partition of India into two countries and the subsequent bloodbath, in retrospect, was there any way out of that?

I think so. When two communities have actually coexisted with each other for seven hundred years, it is impossible not to find ways out of separation. I just don't understand why the leadership of India, both Muslim and Hindu, and including Gandhi, failed to ensure India its historical continuity of two communities, one Hindu and the other Muslim, continuing to live side by side. There were tensions in this relationship, as there are tensions in all relationships. But by and large these two peoples had lived collaboratively with each other, and in the process a lot of things had grown. A civilization had grown. Urdu, a new language, had emerged that was syncretic of what Muslims brought and what they found in the subcontinent. It became a common language of communication. New art forms and a new sort of music had emerged. Northern Indian music is quite different from the old southern Karnatic tradition.

Partition could have been avoided. But as the great poet and writer Rabindranath Tagore had foreseen, not unless Indian anti-imperialist movements also understood the necessity of avoiding the ideology of nationalism. We rejected Western imperialism, but in the process we embraced Western nationalism lock, stock, and barrel.

Nationalism is an ideology of difference. Therefore, Gandhi is at least as responsible for contributing to the division of India as anyone, including Muhammad Ali Jinnah, the founder of Pakistan, if not more so. There is a remarkable conversation that is now available to us between Tagore and Gandhi with Tagore warning Gandhi, "Look, the politics that you are introducing in India is going to divide the two communities."[1]

What about Gandhi's use of Hindu terminology and the trappings of Hinduism and concepts such as Ram Rajya *(the rule of Ram) and his use of* bhajans, *devotional music. Do you think that contributed to a sense of unease among certain Muslims?*

It did. But lest Gandhi is understood as a sort of Hindu communalist, which is the Pakistani nationalist line against him, I should say that he was above all an anti-imperialist opportunist. It is that streak of opportunism in Mahatma Gandhi that led him to pursue a politics that spiritualized and sectarianized the politics of India. Let me give you two examples.

Gandhi on his return to India from South Africa in 1915 was already deeply committed to a policy of passive resistance. The ideas of *ahimsa*, nonviolence, and *satyagraha*, passive resistance, had already developed in his mind during his years in South Africa. So, he arrives in India and hits the national scene with meteoric effect. His rise was dramatic. By 1916, Gandhi was already a national figure.

The first major cause he picked up was saving the caliphate in Turkey. It's one of the spookiest moments in modern Indian history. There in the Middle East, the Ottomans are falling apart. Turkish nationalism, led by the Young Turks and finally by Kemal Ataturk, has no use for the Ottoman sultan. They are throwing the sultanate away. In India, Muslims portray the collapse of the Ottoman sultanate as a product of British machinations. They start an anti-British movement in the name of saving the caliphate in Turkey. Mahatma Gandhi jumps into the fray. You have this massive movement in which Muslims are totally mobilized and Gandhi is leading it along with the Ali brothers, Muhammad and Shaukat, and the Congress Party has thrown its support in behalf of the caliphate movement. Maulana Abdul Kalam Azad, who would later become a major figure in the Indian National Congress, also becomes a leader in this movement. Jinnah warns Gandhi, "Don't do this. This is using religion in politics. This is using religion or appeals of religion to mobilize against the British. One day it will backfire on us." He used that famous phrase: "Mr. Gandhi is spiritualizing Indian nationalist politics."

Later on, Gandhi takes on all these Hindu symbols. Not because they're Hindu symbols but because they were the symbols of the majority people. Therefore, they had the most power to mobilize. In the process, the Muslim community got very frightened that its own cultural traditions and the common culture that was being produced was being shunted aside. It wasn't so much because Gandhi was a Hindu or a communalist, but because he was an anti-imperialist opportunist who would do anything within the framework of his nonviolent philosophy that would mobilize the masses.

It seems to be a harbinger of things to come as well and has an enormous contradiction inherent in it, in that Gandhi on one hand is a critic of one imperial system, the British Raj, yet he is supporting a decaying and disintegrating other imperial system, the Turkish Ottoman Empire. How was he going to undermine the British Raj by supporting another imperial construct?

He would undermine the British Raj by getting the Muslim population of India mobilized, knowing that Hindu-Muslim unity was very central to the success of the anti-colonial movement. To him this was a moment to speak on behalf of an issue that had captured the Muslim imagination to show to the Muslims of India, "Look, we are on your side, too. I can support your cause." What he was not thinking of . . . was the long term. What would be the impact of this? Jinnah did think of it. . . .

Tagore felt, for example, that Gandhi's non-cooperation movement would also tend to divide the Hindus from the Muslims, that it would create deep fissures in Indian society. You can see Tagore's thinking in his novel *The Home and the World*, which Satyajit Ray made into a film with the same title.[2]

In 1920, Tagore argued that nationalism tends to create emotions of exclusion and separation based on differences and not commonality. Nonviolence as an organized, emotive drawing on religious symbolism would also divide and sow seeds of violence in India. So the roots of violence would lie in the very nonviolence that Gandhi was mobilizing on such a large scale. So Gandhi's non-cooperation movement, the burning of imported goods, would hit classes unequally. Poor Muslims in Bengal would be hit differently from middle-class Hindus who dominate Bengal.

In mid-July 1921, the two men met in Tagore's house in Calcutta. Gandhi says, "But Gurudev, I have already achieved Hindu-Muslim unity." Tagore replies, "When the British either walk out or are driven out by us nationalists, what will happen then?" Gandhi: "But Gurudev, my program for winning *swaraj* [self-rule] is based on the principle of nonviolence." Tagore: "Come, Gandhiji, come. Look over the edge of my veranda. Look down there and see what your so-called nonviolent followers are up to." Then he shows him the bazaar where clothes are being burned by the non-cooperation activists. Tagore asks: "Do you think you can hold our violent emotions with your nonviolent principles? No, I don't think so. You know you can't." On these themes he would go on arguing for the next two years with Gandhi.

What happened twenty-six years later, in 1947, was in some remarkably prescient ways seen by Tagore as coming. The poet knew better than the Mahatma.

Nevertheless Gandhi and his movement were able to attract some prominent Muslims. For example, you just mentioned Azad. There were Badshah Khan and others. What accounts for this?

First of all, the most religious Muslim leaders remained on the side of the Indian National Congress and Gandhi. In addition to Maulana Azad, there was Maulana Hussain Ahmed Madani. These were all great religious scholars. It would remain an ironic and relatively unexplained fact of modern Indian history that the idea of Pakistan was very strongly opposed by the Islamic religious scholars of India. The reason for that was, among others, an argument on the part of the *ulema*, the religious scholars of Islam in India, that nationalism was an anti-Islamic ideology, because nationalism proceeds to create boundaries where Islam is a faith without boundaries. It interferes with the universalism that is the

Koranic commitment of Islam. It is a universal religion that will not be subject to drawn boundaries.

Second was a class problem. Most of the proponents of Muslim nationalism, of Pakistani nationalism, were westernized, middle-class people. The *ulema*, the religious leadership, was threatened by the rise of this middle class, which in terms of class, educational outlook, training, and culture was different from them. So they tended to separate from it.

If Gandhi were the sectarian symbol of the Indian Congress Party, would it be fair to characterize Jawaharlal Nehru as its secular leader?

Gandhi was neither sectarian nor a symbol of sectarianism. Some of Gandhi's politics, some of the culture that he produced, unconsciously, unknowingly, and unintentionally contributed to the rise of sectarianism, both on the Muslim side and on the Hindu side. He himself was never party to it. Sectarians on both sides, Hindu as well as Muslim, hated him because they saw him as a universal figure. Gandhi was murdered by a member of a militant Hindu fundamentalist party, Rashtriya Swayamsevak Sangh. While Gandhi dies saying, "*Hé, Ram*" ["Oh, God"], he was killed by a man who thought he was following Ram.

Nehru was a highly westernized nationalist leader, fairly clearly committed to a secular India under the Indian National Congress. I have deep respect for Nehru as a person. Having said that, I think we have to admit that under Nehru a couple of things happened which I had expected him to avoid.

India's president in those early days, Rajendra Prasad, took upon himself to revive, rebuild, and celebrate the reopening of the temple in Somnath in the state of Gujarat. It had been destroyed by Afghan invaders in the tenth century. Nehru went along with it. He shouldn't have. It's not the business of the state to start correcting historical wrongs done a thousand or two thousand years ago. It's not the business of the state to correct historical rights and wrongs of a religious nature.

I didn't realize this phenomenon until almost 1990. I was researching what would become an extraordinary event in Ayodhya in Uttar Pradesh in 1992, the destruction of the historic Babari mosque. The militants who were proceeding to destroy the Babari mosque continued to remind me that this had been done by the Congress Party, too, correcting historical rights and wrongs in the rebuilding of the temple at Somnath.

What's going on in the pre-1947 period in terms of British imperial machinations? Are they seeking to rule by dividing the communities?

That's the nationalist argument and belief, that Britain actually sought and helped divide India between Pakistan and India. I do not read the history that way. The British did divide India along communal lines, especially between 1757 and 1920. Therefore, no actual break occurs in Britain's overall posture of divided rule. It continued. Separate electorates were established. When Muslims would resist British rule, as they did between 1757 and 1857, they were discriminated against in favor of bringing up Hindus. When Congress became organized, more Hindu nationalist figures were there than Muslim ones. Then they favored Muslims against the Congress. So there was a whole set of divide-and-rule policies that the British followed for nearly two centuries.

I don't think it extended, though, to actually choosing to draw the line between Pakistan and India. What happened is that you had a succession of two viceroys. Lord Wavell came in first and soon was recalled and replaced by Lord Louis Mountbatten. Wavell appears to have made the needed moves to save some sort of unity of India under some agreement between the Muslim League and the Congress. Mountbatten, who was the next choice of Britain's Labor government, really carried out a policy of speeding up the division of India without waiting to see if it could be saved or whether the bloodshed that everybody expected to occur could be avoided. Why did he precipitate partition of India? It's an interesting question. I have not been able to find enough material to disprove the British thesis that he was driven by personal ambition more than British policy. But the truth remains that Britain's policy first created the basis for the division of India, a policy of divide and rule over a long period of time, and when the crisis came to a head, Britain did very little to save the unity of India.

Just to back up a little bit chronologically, what kind of impact did German and Japanese attacks on British power during World War II have on the nationalist movement? Did this prove to Indian nationalists that the empire was vulnerable?

Not really. A bigger impact than World War II was the 1904–1905 Russo-Japanese war.

That's Tagore's position.

It's Tagore's position also. The Russo-Japanese war was the first war in a hundred years in which a non-Western army had thoroughly defeated a Western one. Japan defeated Russia. People had for about a hundred years been told with the massive weight of literature, songs, novels, everything, that they were colonized because they were inferior. They were colonized because they were racially backward, because they were scientifically backward, because they were organizationally backward, because they were backward in their knowledge of warfare and strategy and tactics and weaponry. Then suddenly seeing that an Asian power had turned around and beaten a Western power, that had an impact. Lord Curzon was then the viceroy in India. In his memorandum to Downing Street, he wrote that the reverberations of Japan's victory over Russia were like a thunderclap through the whispering galleries of the East.

World War I had a huge impact. India fought on the British side. Our soldiers fought bravely. They fought on the European front. They experienced on the battlefield two things: their equality with British and European soldiers, and the practice of inequality on the part of the empire. On the battlefield they were every day recognizing that they were equals, but they were also experiencing patterns of racial discrimination. Therefore they came back from World War I burning with anger. They and their relatives in many ways gave the push to the nationalist movement. The mass sympathy with the nationalist movement in India occured after World War I.

Let's jump now to August 1942, when Gandhi launches the Quit India campaign. There would be no more cooperation. India would not support the British effort to defeat Germany and Japan. Churchill is the prime minister. He responds to the announcement with: "I have not become His Majesty's First Minister to preside over the liquidation of the British Empire to a half-naked Indian fakir," referring to Gandhi. Why this is so crucial is that the entire Congress leadership is incarcerated, leaving the field open to Jinnah.

It's even more than that. In retrospect it seems to me that the Indian National Congress, and especially Mahatmaji, committed a blunder. Nineteen forty-two was a very difficult year for Britain. London was under heavy bombing. The British fight against fascism was at its climax. It was fairly touch and go. Japan had invaded India. One member of the Congress leadership, Subhash Chandra Bose, had already gone over to the Axis and was organizing an Indian National Army under the Japanese flag.

Gandhi and the Congress leaders were totally justified in saying to Britain, "We will support the war effort, but in return you must give us a promise of independence after the war." But insofar as Britain was not willing to concede that, it was a tactical blunder to have launched the Quit India movement.

Jinnah, who was then the leader of the Muslim League, simply refused to go along. He did so for two reasons. Number one, he was a die-hard anti-fascist. Jinnah couldn't imagine—he was also more Anglicized than Gandhi—doing anything that would hurt the British at that particular moment. And secondly, Jinnah was also very opportunistic. This was for him an opportunity to get British support for his demand for Pakistan. Britain had not been terribly kind towards him before. So on both counts, Congress made a mistake.

Jinnah, as represented in the book Freedom at Midnight *and the film* Gandhi,[3] *comes over as a dark, unsympathetic character.*

So far, publicists, I wouldn't say historians, have been very unkind to Jinnah. He remains the victim, even today, of polemic on the one hand and of the failure of successive Pakistani leaders who have made a mess of Pakistan as a country. Jinnah was not the kind of visionary that Gandhi was. Nor the kind of attractive, tender, cultured, literary, good-looking, emotionally volatile personality that Nehru was. Jinnah had none of that. Jinnah was a Cartesian, Victorian, and urban barrister who was deeply committed to constitutionalism . . . and to rational discourse and politics. He was somewhat distant from the masses. Jinnah was very much like most of his British contemporaries, a liberal constitutionalist. What is really interesting about him is the passage that he makes from a very deeply committed secular nationalist politician whose role in the Indian National Congress was so key that all of them used to describe him as the "ambassador of Hindu-Muslim unity." By 1933, he had become a proponent of Muslim interests only, and then as late as 1940 he launched the demand of Pakistan and seven years later actually achieved it. What is forgotten about him is that in all but eight years of his life he was committed to the unity of India.

Jinnah becomes the first president of independent Pakistan. Not longer after that, he dies.

It was about a year later. He was very sick and was dying of cancer. But everything that he had said and done during that year suggests—and this is a point I have been making a great deal in Pakistan—a vision of Pakistan as having open borders with India. It suggests a vision of Pakistan at peace with all its neighbors. I don't think he imagined what has happened now. To give you a little interesting aside on this: Jinnah was a very rich man. He was a very successful lawyer. For about seventeen years he practiced in England and made a lot of money. In his will, which he drafted, most of his money went to Indian institutions and very little to Pakistani ones. That's an interesting fact.

Jinnah was a remarkably careful investor. Surprisingly, all the investments he made during 1945 to 1947—except two, a small property in Lahore and a big but relatively inexpensive property in Karachi—were in India, not in Pakistan, in areas or in companies that would become Indian and not Pakistani, even in his own imagination. So he was a more interesting figure than propagandists have made him to be. Stanley Wolpert's biography of Jinnah is very good.[4]

What's your assessment of Muhammad Iqbal, the poet and philosopher? He died in 1938. In Pakistan he is celebrated as the national poet.

Muhammad Iqbal was unquestionably a genius and a great poet. He brought Urdu poetry and to a lesser extent Persian poetry into history. Before Iqbal, Urdu and even Persian poetry belonged in the domain of literature, separated from history, and had but a tangential linkage to it. Iqbal brings Urdu into history, and in that sense somebody like Faiz Ahmed Faiz, who died in 1984, is a successor poet.

There is a second great quality to him. He turns, he gives, he stretches, not as much as Faiz would later do, the Urdu language and Urdu poetry. He not only changes its subject into social subjects, subjects other than love, but he changes to some extent its structure. He invests it with power, with anger, with emotion other than that of love. In that sense he broadens the scope of Urdu's poetic discourse.

He is also an original thinker, very much in the German tradition. But his philosophical outlook is not quite as interesting as the fact that he is one of the last great mystics. And his mystical poetry I think will last a very long time.

Recently I was doing a documentary on nationalism for the BBC.[5] I had wanted to put in one segment that doesn't appear actually in the film, unfortunately, which is that Iqbal Day in Pakistan is celebrated officially as the founder's day, precisely because he is projected as the man who conceptualized Pakistan. He's the founding father in some ways. He imagined Pakistan before Jinnah thought of it.

At the same time he's the poet who said, "Sare Jahan Se Achcha Hindustan Hamara."[6] "*In the whole world there is no country better than our India.*"

Exactly. But you have this phenomenon of his being portrayed in Pakistan as the father of Pakistani nationalism. In India, on Republic Day, January 26, the Indian army beat the retreat to *"Sare Jahan Se Achcha."* And the Indian Parliament, I am told, failed to adopt it as the national anthem by two votes. So India ended up with a Tagore song as its national anthem. Bangladesh also ended up with a Tagore song as its national anthem. So Tagore, an anti-nationalist, ended up providing the national anthem to two countries of South Asia. Iqbal has ended up as providing no national anthem whatsoever, because the only one that he wrote that could have been adopted would have been India's.

Back to the politics of India and partition. Are there any analogies to be drawn between the British withdrawing, as you suggest, rather abruptly, from the subcontinent and withdrawing from Palestine, withdrawing from Ireland and in each case leaving a very unhappy and problematic political legacy.

So little has been written on this. My sense is that World War II exhausted Britain's imperial will. There is a lot of speculation . . . in the Middle East and India and Pakistan about the extent to which Britain planned its withdrawal and the ways in which it wished to hand things over to America and play second fiddle to American imperialism, using the United States as a kind of proxy. I don't believe so.

From 1914 to 1939, you begin to notice a holding pattern. It is a desire to keep what you have by partly manipulating reality and partly brute force. . . . Britain doggedly controlled the areas where energy resources were concentrated, because coal had already become completely unimportant to their economy and to power, and in World Wars I and II they had come to a rather deep, respectful realization of the importance of oil. They seemed to care about two things: oil and English people. So, wherever there was a large English colony, such as Kenya, they hung on.

Where there was oil, they hung on. Places like India, they cared much less about.

I have this vivid memory of my brothers saying in 1946 that the worst that can happen would be for the British—these were all nationalists, you understand—to pull out prematurely, not because they were going to give us independence, but they did not even have the staying power to ensure an orderly withdrawal. What we witnessed in 1947 and then again in 1948 was a hurried, unthought-out, irresponsible, and frankly cowardly withdrawal.

Is there any reliable figure on the number of people that perished during the partition of 1947?

No reliable figures. What we do have is an idea that the original estimations were wrong. Originally it was said that four or five million died. No. The number of deaths was minimal in view of the size of the catastrophe. Less than half a million died. But remember, twenty-two million people were displaced, moved from one place to another. To date it remains the largest migration in recorded history.

THE STRUGGLE OVER KASHMIR

That legacy lives on in the subcontinent with wars and an arms race and the ever-vexing issue of Kashmir.

Three wars: 1948, 1965, and then again in 1971 to 1972. Continued conflict over Kashmir, which is costing the Kashmiri people enormously. . . . Continued arms race, which is now nuclear. And worse: India and Pakistan are both now engaged in missile development. The logic of proliferation and the arms race becomes much worse with missiles. Because you can produce one family after another of more advanced, more powerful, longer ranged, blah, blah, blah missiles.

But you know, something that is not often recognized . . . is how these migrations between India and Pakistan have produced communities which are still struggling to settle and come to peace with their new surroundings. It created an environment of social conflict.

The Indian government steadfastly refuses to acknowledge the right of Kashmiris to self-determination. They say that issue was settled in 1947, when the Maharaja of Kashmir acceded to the Indian Union.

That's the official position of India. Pakistan has a similar one, but with much less lethal effect. The Pakistan government's position is that the Kashmiris were given the right to exercise their self-determination by choosing between India and Pakistan. This right was written into the United Nations Security Council resolution of 1948. So Pakistan is insisting that there should be a referendum or a plebescite on the basis of the U.N. resolution, which would force the Kashmiris to choose between India and Pakistan.

Fifty years later the Kashmiris are more interested in choosing either maximum autonomy from these two countries or independence from them. Pakistan is not conceding that. The difference in the Pakistani and Indian position is that India is occupying the Kashmir Valley. There is a revolt, since 1989. So far about 50,000 people have been killed, mostly at the hands of the Indian military. India's denial is costing lives and properties, while Pakistan's old position is not quite as costly but is still outdated. I've been arguing in favor of both India and Pakistan coming to an agreement to give the Kashmiris a chance to decide their future. It can be done in such a way that it does not hurt the interests of either Pakistan or India.

Nehru agreed to hold a plebiscite but then never followed through. There were delays and delays and then it never happened.

Under Prime Minister Nehru, India had committed itself to holding a plebiscite and carrying out the U.N. resolution. That promise India has reneged on.

Comment on the issue of linguistic nationalism in Pakistan and India. In Pakistan there has been the introduction of more Persian and Arabic words and terms. In India the common language is being replaced by a more Sanskritized Hindi.

Less and less so. But what you have observed is absolutely correct for the first twenty years of independence. Nationalism was trying to create new realities, and it had not succeeded very well. First of all, Pakistani nationalism identified Urdu as its national language, thus causing a major problem. . . . Between 1947 and 1970, more than half of the country was Bengali-speaking, in East Pakistan. Bengali was a developed language, at least as developed as Urdu. It produced such great poets as Tagore and such great novelists as Bankim Chandra Chatterjee. Bengalis wanted to keep their own language. As a result, when the Pakistan government, dominated by *mohajir* Urdu-speakers, tried to impose Urdu as the national language, Bengal resisted. Far from strengthening Pakistani nationalism, the imposition of Urdu as a national language actually divided the country. It broke up the unity of Pakistan. It contributed to the separation of Bangladesh as an independent country.

Similarly, in India, Urdu has been identified as a Muslim language, and therefore an effort has been made to use more and more Sanskrit words in the old Hindustani. It doesn't work either, because the absolute truth about Urdu is that it is not a Muslim or a Hindu language. It developed in response to the necessity of two people to discover a common language. It developed out of an honest, genuine, meaningful, creative encounter between Islam and India. Out of that multicultural, multi-religious encounter developed a language that is our common heritage. We call it Urdu in Pakistan. It is called Hindustani in India. What I find interesting is that this language has suffered deeply from the patronage of the state in Pakistan. Witness the resistance of Sindhis to Urdu, of Bengalis to Urdu to the point where they have actually separated. In India it is rooted in the creation of an official language, Hindi, which doesn't appeal to the hearts of people. The result is that in both countries it has suffered. In India it has suffered from official hostility. In Pakistan this language has suffered from official patronage. And at the base this language is now going through a certain transformation in both India and Pakistan.

For example, Urdu is more widely spoken in Pakistan, but it is different from Radio Pakistan's Urdu. Its genius is its syncretic structure. It has now taken on Punjabi, Sindhi, Baluchi, and a huge number of English words and absorbed them within itself. Thus it is now functioning as the language of the Pakistani market. While it is dying as a literary language in schools and universities, it is expanding as a spoken language among common people. In India, Urdu is making a massive comeback through so-called Bollywood films. Bombay films, looking for markets, use Urdu. The songs are all in Urdu. The dialogue is in Urdu. So in a very genuine sense, while officials have created myths of nationalist languages, the people are once again creating languages that are more common between India and Pakistan.

Coming back to Kashmir, what solutions would you propose?

I have argued at some length that India and Pakistan must begin the process of finding a solution with the leaders of the Kashmiri movement. Having said that, we need to recall a little bit of the background.

Kashmir, since 1948, has been divided between India and Pakistan. On the Pakistani side is primarily a Punjabi-speaking area which we call Azad Kashmir, "Free Kashmir," with its capital in Muzaffarabad. It has its own autonomous government, and it does exercise autonomy over local matters. Pakistan almost totally controls its foreign policy, defense, and commercial policies. So in a sense its autonomy is very severely compromised.

India controls all of the rest of Kashmir, which divides into three broad parts. There is the valley. Eighty to eighty-five percent of the valley's population is Muslim. They have over the last two centuries suffered great discrimination, injustice, and oppression at the hands of the *maharaja* of Kashmir put in power by the British. Both regimes were genuinely discriminatory, to the point where Muslims were really serfs. They couldn't join any government services. They were not allowed to study. It was very bad. Since 1948, the situation has improved. More Kashmiris have gone to schools and been educated. A sort of Kashmiri nationalism is centered in the valley with its population of about four million. The valley is one identifiable unique component of Kashmir which is the seat of *Kashmiriat*, Kashmiri nationalism, Kashmiri aspirations.

Then you have Ladakh, which is predominantly Buddhist. Some portions of it are Muslim. India considers Ladakh to be terribly important for its defense because it is next to China. Then there is the large district of Jammu, where roughly 60 percent of the population is non-Kashmiri-speaking Hindus. I think their religion is less important than their ethnicity—they are Dogras, the same people as the maharaja. They have been favored. They speak a different language, Dogri. They feel much closer to India. They do not share the premises of *Kashmiriat*.

Now keep this division in mind. Kashmir is divided between Pakistan and India. The part under India is the most disputed at the moment. That's where the uprising is, and that divides into three parts: the valley, Ladakh, and Jammu. My proposal is that we seek an agreement which leaves the Pakistani part under Pakistani control. Jammu and Ladakh, which do not share the premises of Kashmiri nationalism, should be left under Indian sovereignty. The valley should be given independence. But the agreement among the three—Kashmiri leadership, Pakistan, and India—must envisage uniting Kashmir with divided sovereignty. Unite the territory, keep sovereignties divided, which in our time is fairly possible. Remove the lines of control, remove border patrols, make trade free among these three, make India, Pakistan, and the independent Kashmiri government jointly responsible for the defense of this mountain area.

Kashmir at the moment is a bone of contention between Pakistan and India on the one hand, Kashmiri nationalism in India on the other hand, between Dogras and Kashmiris on yet another hand, and anxieties and fears among Buddhists and Kashmiris on still yet another hand. My proposal would create, instead of a bone of contention, a bridge of peace. Allow each community maximum autonomy with divided sovereignty.

Kashmir would then serve as the starting point of normalizing relations between India and Pakistan. And if India and Pakistan normalize relations, with free trade, free exchange of professionals, and reduction in our arms spending, in ten years we will start looking like East Asia. We are competing with each other with so little money. Four hundred million people in India out of a population of 950 million are living below the poverty line. . . . This condition has to be removed.

Do you think the resolution of the Kashmir dispute could provide that opening to heal the wounds between Pakistan and India?

They can reach agreements on more important issues than Kashmir. Kashmir is more of an emotional issue.

The division of water, of our rivers, was a much more central issue, because that's the lifeline of Pakistan and of the Indian part of Punjab and Haryana. But we reached an agreement on water, the 1960 Indus Basin Water Treaty, years ago, and we have honored it. The World Bank played a very central role in bringing about the treaty, one of the few good things that the World Bank has ever done. Today we are not fighting over water any more. In 1996, India and Bangladesh reached a water agreement on the Ganges.[7]

Except for the die-hard Hindu nationalists in India and the militant Islamic parties in Pakistan, there is no rancor among secular people or among common people between India and Pakistan. In fact, the longer we delay normalization of relations between India and Pakistan and the resolution of the Kashmir conflict, the more we are creating an environment for the spread of Islamic and Hindu militancy.

HIGHER EDUCATION

Tell me about your efforts to establish an independent educational institution in Islamabad.

Higher education in Pakistan has almost totally collapsed. Higher education has collapsed or is collapsing in most third-world countries, including India. In India a sort of effort was made to produce technical education of high quality by the founding of the six Institutes of Indian Technology. There, no humanities, no social sciences are taught. They prepare engineers and a few scientists. Otherwise, the quality of education in India has really drastically declined.

The reasons for the decline of higher education are multiple. One has been the confused and in some ways very uncreative attitude of nationalist governments toward language. On the one hand, these post-colonial states want to impose linguistic orthodoxy suitable to the nationalist mythology. In Pakistani nationalist mythology Urdu, of a Persianized variety, is our official language. In India it is Hindi, of a Sanskritized variety. In Algeria it is Arabic. These are the requirements of the nationalist orthodoxy on the one hand. On the other hand, these are all countries that are organically linked to the capitalist market, meaning they are linked to the imperial metropolis, old or new, either Britain or America, France or America. The result is that they have two sets of standards, one real, the other theoretical.

In Algeria, higher education is supposed to have Arabized. The reality was, the Algerian independent state remained organically tied to France and to the international market. Therefore the local language, Arabic, was devalued. So you have a situation in which you have higher education without a language. You can't impart higher education without a consistent language policy. That contributed to a decline in education.

Second, we all inherited a colonial system of higher education. These post-colonial governments had no will or desire to introduce an alternative system of education. The rhetoric and the structure they announced was that of independence. The reality was that of higher education based on colonial premises and systems. The educational system in this new setting of post-colonial statehood became increasingly dysfunctional because it came under opposing, contradictory pressures.

Third, the functions of colonial education were different. As Lord Macaulay put it, "We want to train in schools of higher learning Indians who would be good at mediating between the Raj and the population, the large majority of Her Majesty's subjects."[8] So, this education was supposed to produce not governors or citizens or educators or administrators of an independent state. It was all meant to produce servants of the empire. This we have continued to do to this day. But that is not the expectation from the educational system. Therefore there is this increasing disjunction between expectation and reality.

Finally I should mention the World Bank, which by and large defines the preferences of post-colonial states. It discourages investments in higher education. The World Bank's line is that third-world countries don't need higher education, they need more literacy. Its policies are aimed at producing a relatively more skilled pool of workers and not people who can govern themselves.

In Pakistan, Prime Minister Zulfikar Ali Bhutto nationalized all the institutions. This meant bureaucrats started running universities. Police officers make really bad presidents of universities. Ditto army officers. Then Mr. Bhutto was followed by General Muhammad Zia ul-Haq. He needed a constituency. He had none. He needed support of a party. No party was willing to support him except Jamat-e-Islami, which charged a fee: Islamization of higher educational institutions. During the pro-western government of Zia ul-Haq, physics professors could not be appointed if they could not name the wives of the Holy Prophet.

Khaldunia, which is the name of the university I'm trying to establish, aims at reviving higher education in one third-world country. It can't revive it on its own. It simply can set some examples and show what kind of curriculum should be the curriculum of an independent, self-governing people. It would make an effort to establish some linkages between the past and the future, some congruence between inherited traditions and contemporary knowledge.

What kind of allies do you have inside and outside of Pakistan helping you on this project?

Outside Pakistan are mostly young academics, mostly from the third world, who are living in the United States or in Europe . . . who want to build a third-world institution. I have received something like 150 letters from qualified young people saying, "We read on the Internet about your efforts. We read a story in the *Chronicle of Higher Education*.[9] If we can help, if we can teach, please let us know. Here is my résumé." So there is that. I have not yet really gone in any serious way to Western funding sources. In Pakistan, very little sympathy or help has come from the landed elite.

That's doesn't surprise you, does it?

No. The Harvard- and Oxford-educated members of Benazir Bhutto's government were the most hostile to my efforts. The business community, especially of Karachi, and also of Punjab, has been supportive.

We have colleges and universities that are graduating ignorants. So you have people with B.A. and M.A. degrees who cannot pass the freshman entrance test at MIT or Harvard or Amherst College. They have actually been given those tests and they can't pass them. So the business house says, "Look, we have a huge number of B.A.s and M.A.S here, but they're not employable. They have no skills. They have no knowledge. They are not trained for anything. So why should we employ them?" The World Bank says, "Look how many unemployed graduates you have. So what's the point of your having higher education?" It's the same argument.

The business community has been very supportive because they need trained hands, leadership, and leadership comes from higher liberal arts education.

And I take it that it's named after Ibn Khaldun, the great Arab scholar?

Abdul-Rahman Ibn Khaldun was a fourteenth-century historian and a sociologist. He's a secular and a scientific figure. He was probably born in Tunis. He grew up in Seville in Spain. He worked, among other places, in Seville, Granada, and in Egypt. He possibly traveled to other parts of the Muslim world. So he's a rather universal figure.

The reason I have picked to name this university after him is my belief that the Muslim people, or for that matter any people in the world, will not make a passage from a pre-industrial traditional culture and economy to a modern culture and economy without finding a linkage within, finding forms and relationships that are congruent between modernity and inherited traditions. . . . My argument is that we will not be able to fight fundamentalism until we produce a modern progressive secular educated class of people who know the traditions and take the best of it.

FRANTZ FANON, MALCOLM X, NOAM CHOMSKY, AND EDWARD W. SAID

In the course of your life you've had some interesting encounters with some rather remarkable figures such as Frantz Fanon in Algeria.

When I met Fanon, he didn't know yet that he had leukemia, but he knew that he was not well. Within months the leukemia was diagnosed, and after that he was racing to eke out the last drops he could get out of his life. *The Wretched of the Earth* was written in a really great hurry.[10] Algeria transformed Fanon in many ways.

From time to time in the late 1960s, I began to see a certain parallel in the lives of Frantz Fanon and Malcolm X. They were two very different personalities by class and educational background. Fanon was a highly educated man. Malcolm had no education. What struck me is that both attained their political consciousness through racial discrimination. It was a consciousness of race and racism of which they were recipients in white-dominated societies that first politicized them. Their first politics was one of sheer anger and reaction to racism, even amounting to separatism. Both discover the universal in humankind through struggle. It is only by entering the process of resistance that they rise above race in their comprehension of social realities and political struggles. And both begin to see class as more central to defining social and human behavior than race. So ultimately both begin to grasp two things: collectives of oppressed people discover themselves, their strengths and their humanity, through struggle. If you don't resist, you don't struggle, you don't discover it. You don't even discover your own humanity, much less that of others.

Both discovered the importance of class and class relationships in the making of societies. The point about Fanon's chapter on violence, for example, in *The Wretched* was massively misunderstood and distorted by the reviewers in the United States and also in Europe. They merely saw in it a celebration of violence, which it was not. What it was was an emphasis on the importance of resistance, of struggle in the discovery of one's own and the other's humanity, of coming into the fullness of collective self.

A clearer expression of that occurred in Fanon's earlier work, *L'Année Cinquième de la Revolution Algérienne*, which has been published in English as *A Dying Colonialism*,[11] He talks about how the Algerian woman achieves the willingness to give up the veil voluntarily when she enters into a struggle and how the veil becomes a symbol of resistance as long as resistance isn't organized. Clinging to that tradition was the only way they could say no to France and its cultural hegemony.

He does the same thing with the use of radio before and after the Algerian struggle. He shows that the Algerians were rejecting the radio as the instrument of the oppressor, and then they used the radio as an instrument of liberation once they had entered into a struggle. One's relationship to technology, to social customs, to the very symbols of colonialism, of oppression, changes when you enter into struggle. That was the point he was making about violence, not just simply an indulgence in the beauty of it. He was badly misrepresented, I thought.

His enlightening last thoughts in *The Wretched* appeared in the chapter entitled "The Pitfalls of National Consciousness." I still assign that chapter to students when I teach courses on the post-colonial state. He saw with clarity the pitfalls of nationalism, the kind of structure that it will produce, the dependencies that it will develop, the post-colonial state that will be nothing more than a new instrument of imperial domination. He saw it all. And he saw it in the emergence of a collaborative elite which he called "*Les enfants dorés de ligne aérienne.*" These will be the golden-eyed boys of airlines, of the jets. My last thought about Fanon is, I wish he had lived. He was not yet forty when he died.

Did you actually work with him?

I worked closely with him for about six months. He was heading the information office of the the National Liberation Front (FLN) and editing its underground newspaper, *El Moudjahid*.

Any observations on his book Black Skin, White Masks?[12]

If you take *Black Skin, White Masks* and read *A Dying Colonialism* or *The Wretched of the Earth*, or for that matter the editorials that he wrote in *El Moudjahid*, which have been published as *Toward the African Revolution*,[13] you see the passage of Fanon from race to class, from violence to reconstruction of society, from a distant resistance to reconstruction, from reaction to creativity. *Black Skin* is a book of anger at racism, the humiliation, the degradation, the devaluation of personality, of humanity that one suffers. It comes out in Amílcar Cabral, in the early works of Leopold Senghor, and in Malcolm X. Malcolm experiences the same kind of transformation, but through a religious experience. That is to say, the experience of going to Mecca for the pilgrimage. It's quite remarkable. I saw him before he left and after he came back from the pilgrimage, how he had changed.

In Malcolm's case it's been suggested that because of performing the haj *to Mecca that he went from a narrow, nationalist position to one that embraced a global perspective.*

Malcolm was a convert to Nation of Islam racist ideology. In its reaction to the black experience of centuries of white racism that began with slavery, the Nation of Islam rejected the very notion of having anything to do with white people. Nation of Islam was a black nation, not a nation of black, white, and brown people living and working together. It was a black separatist movement. Malcolm X was a minister of separatism.

It was similar to Zionism as an ideology: Jews will be safe and good only if they are able to establish an exclusionary Jewish state. They happen to have done it in Palestine, but it's that same ideology.

Malcolm was such an open-minded person. What he discovered upon going to Mecca was that Islam was a religion that was anti-racist. Here were Turks, Bosnians, Sudanese, Senegalese, Malians, Pakistanis, Chinese, Scots, and all kinds of people, white, black, yellow, brown, all gathered in one place, eating together, living on the same floor, wearing exactly the same *aba* [robe]. It shook him. He said, "There is no race here. What is going on?" When he came back he said, "It is possible. I have seen a society at work which had no consciousness of race."

What he was not fully grasping was that another kind of division was already there—the division of class—which is obliterated during that short pilgrimage during which nobody is allowed to ask, "Are you rich or are you poor?" But that moment to him was quite important. He lost his life as a result.

Incidentally, I met him when I was a student at Princeton. Princeton was the first university in this country, the very first non-black institution to which Malcolm X had come and spoken. I helped organize his visit.

One of the figures who emerges very prominently in the U.S. anti-war movement in the mid-1960s is Noam Chomsky.

In 1964, when the antiwar movement was starting to emerge, he was already a historic figure for his contribution to modern linguistics. . . . In 1967, Chomsky wrote an article in the *New York Review of Books* titled "The Responsibility of Intellectuals."[14] It was a remarkable piece of work that argued most eloquently that the Cold War had ruined the conscience of intellectuals and traditions of knowledge and inquiry in America and killed the absolutely necessary tradition of questioning, of dissent. It was an indictment of the Cold War, of its impact on the intellectual and cultural life of America, and of the intellectuals who fell into this trap. It had a powerful impact.

So, it's then that I came to know of him as an intellectual activist. During that period of the Cold War, two articles had a very important impact on the movement. One was Noam's "Responsibility of Intellectuals." Another was, quite accidentally, I think, a piece I wrote in *The Nation* earlier, in 1965, entitled "How to Tell When the Rebels Have Won."[15] This article argued that the United States had lost the war in Vietnam and from this point on all it could do was to kill and that all the killing it will do will amount to nothing. It had an impact. Senators J. William Fulbright and Frank Church immediately used it in the first Vietnam hearings.

So, I had known of Noam. As I'm talking to you, I cannot recall when I met him. I encountered him very much in the same way a person encounters the wind or the air or the rain. It just happened. It was probably such a natural event in my life that I have no memory of it. Meeting Fanon was not so natural. I can recall the exact time.

Before we met, Chomsky and I had belonged to the same community of intellectuals who were against the war. We had spoken most probably half a dozen times or more on the telephone. Somewhere we met.

In December 1970, after I was arrested on charges of kidnapping Henry Kissinger and so on, I was in jail for a bit and then came out on bail. Noam Chomsky was the second person who had flown to Chicago to see me. He stayed over in my very bare apartment on a wooden platform and didn't complain. We talked a lot. The first one to fly out without having known me too closely, again, just as an anti-war comrade, was Richard Falk from Princeton.

Over the years, Noam and I have become good friends. Unfortunately our lives are so organized that I haven't seen him very much. But occasionally we do get together.

Chomsky has a singular place in the life of dissidence in the United States today. Why do you think his voice now is seemingly more prominent, not in the mainstream media, but more and more people are reading his books and attending his lectures?

Three reasons: persistence, consistency, and independence. Chomsky has never slowed down. He has never lost hope. . . . Once he had identified the beast—imperialism—he has pursued it, no matter what coats the beast wore at any given time. Is it the media, is it militarism, is it intervention, is it globalization?

Second, consistency. He has never wavered. He has never fallen into the trap of saying, "Clinton will do better." Or, "Nixon was bad, but Carter at least had a human rights presidency." There is a consistency of substance, of posture, of outlook in his work. Consistency of course means repetition. Over the last twenty years, Chomsky has repeated himself a lot, something he doesn't quite do in linguistics.

But he is teaching many people. I have yet not learned from him this powerful thing—namely, that truth has to be repeated. It doesn't become stale just because it has been told once. So keep repeating it. Don't bother about who has listened, who has not listened. He knows that the media and the other institutions of power are so powerful that telling the truth once is not enough. You've got to keep repeating different facts, prove the same point.

If you will forgive me for saying it—Chomsky probably wouldn't like this expression, given how secular a man he is—his power of repetition almost resembles a Sufi chant. Sufis have a rule. They discover a principle, and that principle is repeated. The difference is that theirs was a spiritual principle, and his is a secular one. Theirs was for salvation; his is for liberation. The power of repetition is just extraordinary.

Third, independence. Chomsky is not a Trotskyite, a Leninist, or a Maoist. Chomsky is an anarchist humanist who believes that state power concentrated in fewer hands will produce evil.

Edward Said is another figure that you have been involved with over the years. When did you first meet him?

Some time early in 1968, Ibrahim Abu-Lughod had published a magazine called *Arab Affairs*. One article in it struck me as being unusually good. It was by Edward Said. Its title was "The Arab Portrayed."[16] It's a remarkable work of critical reconstruction of what the media and political discourse on the 1967 Arab-Israeli war had done to the Arab as a person and as a people. He connected that to the anti-Semitic discourse of the nineteenth and early twentieth centuries, concluding that today the Arab, the Palestinian particularly, had become the shadow of the Jew.

I called Ibrahim Abu-Lughod and asked him, "Who is this man?" He said, "He's a young man, roughly your age. He teaches English literature at Columbia University." I said, "If you see him, let him know that I really liked his article."

We met in 1968. I recall that incident in the introduction to your book of interviews with Edward.[17]

THE PALESTINIAN QUESTION
This was a period of heightened activity.

There was a big meeting organized by Arabs living in the United States, soon after the emergence of the Palestinian Liberation Organization (PLO). The PLO had fought off an Israeli attack at the Kerameh refugee camp in Jordan. That minor victory in a minor battle assumed a very large meaning in Arab and Palestinian emotion because it had come after the extraordinary defeat in the 1967 war. The great hopes of Palestinian people had become linked to the PLO as an armed liberation movement. That year also marked the climax of the Vietnam War. Armed struggle had reached the height of its appeal in the third world and in left circles around the world.

Some Arab students invited me to give the keynote address at this conference. . . . Some of the PLO leaders were also there. I argued that armed struggle was supremely unsuited to the Palestinian condition, that it was a mistake to put so much emphasis on it. I argued that armed struggle is less about arms and more about organization, that a successful armed struggle proceeds to out-administer the adversary and not out-fight him. And that the task of out-administration was a task of out-legitimizing the enemy. Finally, I argued that this out-administration occurs when you identify the primary contradiction of your adversary and expose that contradiction not only to yourselves, which you don't need to do so much, but to the world at large, and more important, to the people of the adversarial country itself.

I argued that Israel's fundamental contradiction was that it was founded as a symbol of the suffering of humanity . . . at the expense of another people who were innocent of guilt. It's this contradiction that you have to bring out. And you don't bring it out by armed struggle. In fact, you suppress this contradiction by armed struggle. The Israeli

Zionist organizations continue to portray the Jews as victims of Arab violence.

I'm interested that this was what you wanted to project in this conference, coming off your first-hand experience in Algeria where one million Algerians were killed in a revolutionary struggle.

Yes, but precisely because of that. If I hadn't gone through the Algerian experience, I wouldn't have reached this conclusion. After seeing what I saw in Algeria, I couldn't romanticize armed struggle. The costs to the people of Algeria were very high. OK, they agreed to pay the cost, but it was high. Also, I knew what many people would not recognize even today, which is that the Algerians lost the war militarily, but won it politically. They were successful in isolating France morally. So the primary task of revolutionary struggle is to achieve the moral isolation of the adversary in its own eyes and in the eyes of the world. . . .

For example, in 1968 I said, "This is a moment to fit ships in Cyprus, fit boats in Lebanon and say, 'We're not going to destroy Israel. That is not our intent. We just want to go home.' Reverse the symbols of Exodus. See if the Israelis are in a mood to sink some ships. They probably will. Let them do so. Some of us will die. Let us die." . . . When I had finished, there was considerable discomfort on the part of the young Arab students. They were shocked: the expert on guerilla warfare, the man from Algeria, the anti-Vietnam War leader is arguing the exact reverse of what we believe in. They were very gracious, so nobody hooted me or anything, but there was coldness. A man walked up to me and said, "I'm Edward Said. I want to thank you for what you have done." I knew from his article that I was meeting someone who had a very fresh and original mind. Since then we have been very close friends.

Back up a little bit and pursue another line for just a moment. You said you wrote an article for The Nation *in 1965. You were still a young guy. How did you feel in terms of authenticity and authority as someone born in India, migrated to Pakistan, educated in the United States, goes to Algeria, to be talking on these kinds of issues to an American audience? Did you have any hesitation there?*

I never hesitated. . . . I felt that racism was a universal question. And the fight against racism was a universal challenge.

In 1964 or 1965, we had a small meeting of faculty and students. . . . The Tonkin Gulf Resolution had been passed. The Vietnamese had attacked the American base in Pleiku. The bombings of North Vietnam had just started. The process of escalation of the war in Indochina had just begun.

There was some discussion about what we could do. Since we had just come out of the tradition of sit-ins in the civil rights movement and we were living at a time of great conformity to the ideals and assumptions of the Cold War, we felt that a teach-in would be just the thing to do. It would be an act of resistance to tell the truth. . . .

Subsequently I got a visit from the FBI. Two men came. They showed their cards. They first asked me if I was a citizen of the United States. I said, "No." They said, "Don't you feel that as a guest in this country you should not be going about criticizing the host country's government?" I said, "I hear your point, but I do want you to know that while I am not a citizen, I am a taxpayer. And I thought it was a fundamental principle of American democracy that there is no taxation without representation. I have not been represented about this war. And my people, Asian people, are being bombed right now." Surprisingly, the FBI agents looked deeply moved and blushed at my throwing this argument at them. They were speechless. Then I understood something about the importance of having some congruence between American liberal traditions . . . and our rhetoric and tactics.

To further pursue the argument that you were making at the 1968 conference to Arab Americans, liberation struggles need to morally isolate the adversary. I'll give you that, with a qualification: It has to be an adversary that subscribes, at least on a rhetorical level, to liberal democratic traditions.

Obviously, you couldn't morally isolate the regimes of Hitler or Stalin. A strategy of moral isolation assumes that the adversary has based its own legitimacy on moral grounds. Gandhi understood this rather well with regard to British colonialism. He understood the contradiction of British colonialism, which justified itself on liberal principles and was violating them. He stood British imperialism upside down on its head.

At the risk of offending some people, between 1967 and now, Israeli society has in some ways worsened. Likud, a right-wing party that has fewer moral compunctions, has now become the major party and has organized a large right-wing constituency such as . . . the Gush Emunim and other settler movements. They are much less susceptible to moral arguments. Centrist Zionism's primary contradiction was its principles of legitimacy were moral and its practices were immoral. And it is that which had to be fully used. Opportunities were lost in the 1970s, once the PLO had become a quasi-state in Lebanon. An opportunity has returned now, but there are no takers.

Arab governments such as Egypt and Jordan have, for example, committed themselves to peace with Israel. The PLO leadership has committed itself to peace with Israel. The terms of peace have been spelled out in the Oslo agreement. This agreement is extremely unjust, because it doesn't respond to any of the fundamental issues in this conflict. It offers no compensation, no restitution, no return to the half of Palestine's population who are now refugees. It offers no settlement of the issue of water rights in the occupied territories. It offers Palestinians no right to self-determination. It offers Palestinians no protection from expanding Israeli settlements. It offers Palestinians no solution or Arabs generally of the problem of Jerusalem, which is as holy to Muslims and Christians as it is to Jews. So in a very genuine sense, Oslo leaves open all the fundamental questions that have defined the Arab-Israeli conflict.

What it does do is to say there will be no war and the two peoples will deal with each other and settle these issues peacefully. In that situation, the government of Israel is taking every step to violate what little there is in the spirit of Oslo by expanding settlements, by encircling Jerusalem, by even starting buildings in East Jerusalem, and by keeping Israeli forces in the West Bank and Gaza. The Palestinian movement's only gain—if you call it a gain—is that its leadership has returned to the occupied territories. If Yasir Arafat would take on the role of a Gandhi or a Martin Luther King and announce tomorrow, "I must stop these settlements. They violate the spirit of Oslo. We are committed to peace. You are making war. We do not want to use violence against you. Peacefully we will march against you. We will sit in. We will clog the roads, start a full-scale movement, and discipline the Palestinians not even to throw stones, intifada-style, because Israelis will use and justify bullets against stones. They will use soldiers against children. Don't even give them that." Israel will divide. It will divide as a society the way America divided. I would keep it divided until it makes peace.

My argument about what the Palestinian struggle should be about has returned again. But if you don't have a leadership, then what do you do? I have spoken to Arafat about this line in great detail probably five or six times. He always took notes, always promised to do things, always did nothing.

Is it a kind of Leninist, top-down, hierarchical model?

It's hierarchical, but not Leninist. Once we use the word "Leninist," other images come in, such as discipline, austerity, and genuine sacrifice. The PLO took on the slogan of armed struggle, understanding it as merely the use of arms. They took on the slogan of political organization or parallel hierarchy only to distribute patronage. It's a traditional political Arab organization that runs like Tammany Hall in its worst days. Political bosses stay in control by distributing patronage, using gun-toting as a method for legitimation. Their gun-toting stopped once it stopped serving their purpose.

You attended a meeting in New York with Noam Chomsky and Edward Said and top PLO officials.

In 1975 or 1976, several leaders of the PLO, minus Arafat, were in New York for a U.N. session. Ibrahim Abu-Lughod, Edward Said, and the PLO delegation at the U.N. called me and Chomsky and asked if we would come talk to these leaders. We both went and gave them our critique of the movement—its preoccupation with armed struggle and its inability to focus American civil society. In very gentle terms, we offered that the United States is a complex society and should be reached in various ways. We emphasized the importance of its political components, of talking to Israelis, including Israeli intellectuals, those who are questioning, doubting. We talked about the importance of talking to the leadership of the Jewish community here and reaching various wings of American civil society. It required a change in the posture and the rhetoric that was coming out of the PLO's leadership headquarters.

They listened, respectfully. There was one man there, Shafiq al-Hout, who understood and agreed with us. The rest justified their positions. Some gave lectures that were essentially ignorant. Chomsky felt particularly depressed by the encounter. I was beyond depression by that time. I had seen enough. They defeated themselves more than the Israelis did.

It's in the late 1970s that Edward Said joins the Palestine National Council, the Palestinian parliament in exile. Was he voicing those kinds of misgivings and criticisms internally?

Yes. The closest Edward came to publicly criticizing the PLO's strategy, tactics, and politics was in some references in *The Question of Palestine*, which was published in 1979.[18] He questioned the use of violence in the Palestinian struggle, which I thought was very courageous at that time. Said, Abu-Lughod, and Shafiq al-Hout were always very keen to have me speak out to Arafat and other top leaders of the PLO, probably because they felt I would speak bluntly. I had a certain reputation in the Middle East, especially among young people and the intelligentsia, as someone who did not make unprincipled compromises. My integrity was not in question to them. They took me to meet Arafat three or four times. I always spoke out and every time I did, Edward openly supported me. The last time was in Tunis.

In 1980, I had made a second trip to the south of Lebanon, where PLO forces were concentrated. . . . The Israelis had already invaded southern Lebanon in 1978. I saw that they would invade again, because the PLO's posture in Lebanon was much too tempting for an organized army of adversaries. I had written to Arafat saying, "The way you are organized you will not be able to resist for more than five days." In 1982, the invasion came. Nothing surprised me.

After the PLO had been driven out of Lebanon, I went to see Arafat with Edward and Abu-Lughod. The PLO had been beaten and had left for Tunisia. Arafat was lost and depressed and this time incapable of concentrating on listening to me. He made no pretense, for example, of taking notes, like he used to do. It was too late to go on harping on giving up armed struggle and changing tactics. They couldn't change tactics anymore or strategy, but they had given up armed struggle anyway. So, at this point I argued with him that his single biggest need was to develop a really clear-cut position, to remove the question of recognition. Announce that you have no problem recognizing the state of Israel. But ask which Israel you are being asked to recognize. Is it the Israel of 1948? Is it the Israel of the 1947 partition plan? Is it the Israel of 1948 that expanded three times more? Is it the Israel of the 1967 war? Is it the Israel of Israeli imagination? Because Israel is the only country today, the only member of the United Nations, that has refused to announce its boundaries.

I said, "Tell us where your boundaries are. Let's negotiate those boundaries. . . . What are your minimum boundaries of a Palestinian state? Set it down. This is what we want." Develop a viable, acceptable peace proposal that die-hard Zionists may not accept but the world, as well as decent Israeli opinion, could not afford to reject. One that would offer Israel the security that it publicly claims to want, but which insists on justice for the Palestinians in ways that no one could find unreasonable.

I told him he should develop such a five- or six-point proposal, and then base his struggle on it. Fight over it. Mobilize governments around it. Go to the United Nations with it. Go to the United States Congress with it. You may hit a blank wall for a long time, but you will be creating legitimacy for the rights of the Palestinian people for a viable option, and ultimately the Israelis will have to come to the table with you. . . .

When we came out of the meeting, Edward looked literally paper white. He was angry and disappointed. He shook his head. Another person who was with us, a Palestinian banker from Paris, went back and stayed with Arafat for about twenty minutes while we waited outside. He came out also looking downcast and said, "You know I went back to tell Abu Amar [Arafat's *nom de guerre*] that he should listen to Eqbal. If he doesn't listen now, there's no hope for us."

That's the last time I saw Arafat. Israel's government finally gave me a *laissez-passer* in 1994. I went to Gaza first and spoke there to a human rights organization. I sent a message to Arafat saying that I was in Gaza. I didn't ask for an interview. Every time it was his office that had invited me, maybe at somebody else's suggestion. He never even contacted me. On the first day, the hotel where the human rights conference was to be held was told not to allow the conference to meet.

Arafat and the people around him are thugs collaborating with Israel. Right now, in their moment of greatest thuggery, the Western media is saying nothing about them. They have suddenly become good guys.

Why do you think, and you've had more than thirty years examining the Israeli-Palestinian-Arab question, it's been so difficult in the United States for there to be an open dialogue?

I thought the best explanation ever given to this phenomenon was in a chapter of *The Question of Palestine* called "Zionism from the Standpoint of Its Victims."[19] Said argues that the attainment of hegemony of the Zionist discourse—which devalues Palestinian Arab reality—was an aspect of the Orientalist discourse. He demonstrates it in very practical ways. That phenomenon is stronger today, because unlike in 1947 or even 1960, Israel's legitimacy is interwoven with American institutions of power, including the media, the Department of Defense, and the CLA. Israel and the United States are now tied in multiple layers of integrated relationships. In this situation, it's very difficult for any voice to be heard. It is difficult to teach properly, because you start getting calls and harassments of all kinds. I have been very lucky, and that's one of the reasons why I teach in a small college. Hampshire gives me the freedom to do what I want to do outside of the college.

Earlier you said you "paid the price" at Cornell.

I paid very heavy prices over the years, not just at Cornell. I would rather not talk about it. It's McCarthyism of a kind, conformities enforced for the few voices. . . . At the moment, there are four or five people who are foreign affairs columnists of the *New York Times*, the newspaper of record. Two of them, A.M. Rosenthal and William Safire, are right-wing Zionist supporters of the Likud Party. The third is Thomas Friedman, a centrist Zionist supporter of the Israeli Labor Party. A fourth, Anthony Lewis, is a liberal and a putative Zionist. Of all the foreign affairs columnists of the *New York Times*, there is not one that would take an independent position on the issue of the Arab-Israeli conflict, much less . . . one that would comprehend the aspirations, the needs, the feelings of the Arab or Palestinian people. The same pattern is repeated in the *Washington Post*, the *Chicago Tribune*, and other major papers.

In this time of multiculturalism, Rosenthal describes Islam as a "hate civilization" and gets away with it. Simultaneously, Edward Said, Noam Chomsky—I'm a smaller figure, but I've written for the *New York Times* for a long time—none of us can write a word on the Middle East in its pages or in the *Washington Post*. We are not unknown people. We are not bad writers. No, our voices have to be banned. . . .

I don't think it's a question of Jewish control over the media. That's pure nonsense. It's a much more complex system of the exercise of power and hegemony. There are some views that are to be blocked.

I mean, Jesus, what would the world say if the Iranian newspaper of record described Judaism as a "hate civilization"? We would condemn that.

FAIZ AHMED FAIZ

One event I want you to describe is a meeting in Beirut with you, Faiz Ahmed Faiz, and Edward Said.

I think it was 1980. Zia ul-Haq was the military dictator in Pakistan. He was very strongly supported by great human rights worshippers such as the government of the United States and the publishers of the *New York Times*. Faiz Ahmed Faiz had found a sanctuary of sorts in war-torn Beirut. He came to my lecture in Beirut. I noticed him sitting in the back. I went up to him and introduced him to Edward. Edward wrote about it a few years later in an article in *Harper's* entitled "The Mind of Winter: Reflections on Life in Exile."[20] Faiz wrote a number of very moving poems about his experience in Lebanon. Edward had a sense immediately that here was a great poet and therefore showed a great deal of interest in talking and listening to him. At one point, we were having dinner in a restaurant where curfew had already been imposed but we continued to stay on and fighting had begun. Faiz recited several poems as I translated them verbatim. We all ignored the shooting and went on.

Said writes that you stopped translating and the Urdu filled the night air.

I stopped translating at one point. Faiz continued to recite. But, see, Urdu poetry has an extraordinary sound. About a week ago, I did a bilingual reading in Amherst of Faiz's poetry with Agha Shahid Ali. A lot of Americans who know nothing of Urdu had tears in their eyes. Faiz brought the Urdu language from where Muhammad Iqbal had left it right smack at the center of history. He, like Pablo Neruda in Spanish and Nazim Hikmet in Turkish, stretches the Urdu language and establishes extraordinary congruence and harmony, between the new, modern forms, including free verse, with the classical rhymed poetry of Urdu and Persian. It's from that congruence that the popularity and power of Faiz's poetry occurs. Also, of course, the power of his poetry comes from the fact that he was socially and politically a most engaged poet who spent many years in prison.

ORIENTALISM

It seems that one of Said's great contributions is his defining how knowledge was constructed, particularly around the Arab Middle East and Islam, to serve the interests of imperial power. That was first developed in Orientalism *and still further in* Culture and Imperialism.[21]

I would put it slightly differently. I think the greatest singular achievement of Said, as a literary critic, beginning with *Orientalism*, has been to put imperialism at the center of Western civilization. . . . What you find in both historical, political literature and literary works in the West in the last 400 years is a great emphasis on the role of enlightenment in the making of civilization and its discourse. You find a great deal of emphasis on rationalism . . . on democracy and democratic values, and on liberalism, as an aspect of enlightenment. There is an almost remarkable tendency to not mention imperialism as shaping the contours of Western civilization.

In *Orientalism*, Said's argument is not about Orientalists. It is about the relationship of knowledge to power, of culture to imperialism, and of civilization to expansion. He put therefore the whole issue of Western expansion, domination, and imperialism as central forces in defining the nature of civilization itself. That includes music, literature, poetry, politics, and the writing of history. The remarkable thing is that he did it with such power and erudition that no one has successfully challenged his premises.

Have you seen any change in the academy in terms of people who are focused on Islamic civilization, the South, the third world?

There is a change in the academy in the same way as in linguistics. There are two times: before Chomsky and after Chomsky. In literary criticism and historical writing there are two times: before *Orientalism* and after *Orientalism*. There's no question about that. Has it changed the study of Islam in the West? Yes. It has changed both for the better and for the worse.

For example, partly in reaction to Said, but primarily from its own needs and prejudices, there is at the moment an organized attempt to demonize Islam and Muslims. This includes an Orientalist as established and respected as Bernard Lewis, and a polemicist as disrespected as Howard Bloom, who wrote *The Lucifer Principle*. The book's argument is that Islam is a satanic, barbarian civilization.[22]

It's rather interesting to see what the Serbs did with it. They based their whole genocide on this derivative rhetoric that demonizes Islam and Muslims. That is why the Serb fascists have been saying to journalists with a sense of disbelief, "We don't understand why you folks don't understand that we were doing your job. We were ethnically cleansing

Europe. We were doing the job for you. After all, you have all understood . . . that this is a demon religion, a demon civilization."

At the same time, there is a body of scholarly work on Islam, and on Muslims and the Middle East, that shows a kind of understanding that we did not have fifty years ago. . . . But I would say that *Orientalism*'s biggest single impact has been . . . outside of the Islamic purview, because Islamic civilization still remains a target for political reasons. So there the impact has been, ironically, the least. On the history of blacks, Africa, race relations in the United States, and on literary criticism and the historical writings of colonial Western expansion, it has had a big impact.

What about in the third world? Has it been an influence?

Not significantly, I am sorry to say. There is a certain canonization of Said and *Orientalism*, but beyond that, very few critical works of history have appeared from the third world that show genuine learning from the Orientalist construct. The best developments probably have been in Indian historiography at Jawaharlal Nehru University in Delhi and with the subaltern group that started with Ranajit Guha.[23] In Arabic there have been a couple of new things that have come out, including Muhammad Abed al-Jabry's work, that have been interesting, but there's not too much.[24]

THE DEMONIZATION OF ISLAM

Where do you trace chronologically when Islam, Muslims, Arabs become targeted as a threat or an enemy of the West?

This is not a completely new phenomenon. . . . In the tenth century, for the first time you saw a certain notion of demonizing Islam. At that point, it wasn't so misplaced from the European point of view, because Islam was an expansionist civilization, and therefore considered . . . a threat and a menace. The Crusades witnessed the first instance of demonization along religious lines, that is, demonization of Islam itself rather than of Arabs or Turks. . . . Next you notice it in the period when British and later French colonialists encountered Muslim resistance.

There was the case of the Mahdi, who besieged and killed General Charles George Gordon in 1885 in Khartoum. That particular moment saw a great deal of emphasis on Islamic fanaticism. Colonial battles were never remembered unless a Custer was killed or a Gordon besieged. Millions of people may die, but the memories are of Custer and Gordon.

This is the third time . . . in the last 1,400 years that there is this organized attempt to demonize Islam. This time it's more organized and sustained, because the means have changed. Today there is mass communication.

Does this process of demonization come from a shared consensus that is not articulated? Or are people meeting at Harvard and saying, "OK, we have to get together and demonize Arabs and Muslims?"

I don't think there is a conspiracy. . . . Great imperial powers, especially democratic ones, cannot justify themselves on the basis of power or greed alone. No one will buy it. . . . Modern imperialism needed a legitimizing instrument to socialize people into its ethos. To do that it needed two things: a ghost and a mission. The British carried the white man's burden. That was the mission. The French carried *la mission civilisatrice*, the civilizing mission. The Americans had manifest destiny and then the mission of standing watch on the walls of world freedom, in John F. Kennedy's ringing phrase. Each of them had the black, the yellow, and finally the red peril to fight against. There was a ghost and there was a mission. People bought it.

After the Cold War, Western power was deprived both of the mission and the ghost. So the mission has appeared as human rights. It's a very strange mission for a country which for nearly a hundred years has been supporting dictatorships in Latin America and throughout the world. Chomsky and Herman wrote about this in *The Washington Connection and Third World Fascism*.[25]

In search of menace, they have turned to Islam. It's the easiest, because it has a history.

It's also the most vulnerable.

It's vulnerable. It's weak. . . . Islamic countries are home to the oil resources of the West. The West has encountered resistance in Algeria, Egypt, among the Palestinians, and with the Iranian revolution—enough to arouse anxiety that Western interests . . . are threatened. And there is a history of demonization. All these things fall into place. And there are enough vested interests to take advantage of it.

Media coverage of Islamic fundamentalism seems to be very selective. There are certain types that are not discussed at all. For example, the Saudi version, which may he among the most extreme. Americans hear a lot about Hezbollah and Hamas and groups in Egypt, like the Akhwan.

This is a very interesting matter you are raising. . . . Saudi Arabia's Islamic government has been by far the most fundamentalist in the history of Islam. Even today, for example, women drive in Iran. They can't drive in Saudi Arabia. Today, for example, men and women are working in offices together in Iran. Women wear chador, but they work in offices. In Saudi Arabia, they cannot do it. So on the basis of the nature and extent of fundamentalist principles or right-wing ideology, Saudi Arabia is much worse in practice than Iran. But it has been the ally of the United States since 1932, so nobody has questioned it.

But much more than that is involved. Throughout the Cold War, starting in 1945 when it inherited its role as a world power, the United States has seen militant Islam as a counterweight to communist parties in the Muslim world. During this entire period, the Muslim brotherhood in Egypt was not an enemy of the United States. . . . The U.S. government actually promoted and supported the Islamic regime that is now in power in Sudan. General Muhammad Gaafar al-Nimeiry was allied to the Islamic movement of Sudan and was a friend.

America's two major leverages on its allies in Western Europe and Asia—the nuclear umbrella and economic superiority—had drastically diminished by the early 1970s. The U.S. was looking for new leverages over its allies. They picked the Middle East because this was where the energy resources for the industrial economies of Japan and Europe came from. An established, unchallenged American influence in this region . . . could control prices and show Europe and Japan, "We can give you cheap oil. We can make your oil expensive. We hold your economic lifeline."

This was the time of the Nixon Doctrine, namely, the use of regional powers to police the region for the United States. In the Middle East, they chose Iran and Israel. In the Pentagon, throughout most of the 1970s, they were called "our two eyes in the Middle East." In 1978, after having or perhaps because of having taken some $20 billion of military hardware from the United States, the shah of Iran fell under the weight of his own militarization. The 1979 Islamic revolution threatened American interests deeply . . . materializing in an uglier form during the hostage crisis.

Within a year, quite ironically, something totally the opposite happens. The Soviet Union intervened in Afghanistan. In Pakistan, an Islamic fundamentalist dictator promoted, with the help of the CLA, an Islamic fundamentalist resistance against the Soviets in Afghanistan. Now what you had was Islamic fundamentalists of a really hardcore variety, the *mujahideen* in Afghanistan, taking on the "evil empire." They received billions in arms between 1981 and 1988 from the United States alone. Add additional support from Saudi Arabia, under American encouragement. . . . American operatives went about the Muslim world recruiting for the *jihad* in Afghanistan, because the U.S. saw it as an opportunity to mobilize the Muslim world against communism. That opportunity was exploited by recruiting *mujahideen* in Algeria, Sudan, Egypt, Yemen, and Palestine. From everywhere they came. They received training from the CIA. They received arms from the CLA. I have argued in some of my writings that the notion of *jihad* as "just struggle" had not existed in the Muslim world since the tenth century until the United States revived it during its *jihad* against the Soviet Union in Afghanistan.

Since then, almost every Islamic militant, including those in Israel, Algeria, and Egypt . . . has been trained in Afghanistan. The CLA people call it "Islamic blowback."

These are aspects that the American media is not willing to touch on. The *New York Times'* four foreign affairs columnists are neither qualified nor would they want to be qualified to comment on these realities.

What side effects have U.S. support of the mujahideen *had on Pakistani society?*

One is the extraordinary proliferation of drugs and guns. Something like $10 billion in arms was pumped into Pakistan and Afghanistan. Half of it at least rebounded and became part of international trade. Much of it ended up in Pakistan. So, you have a situation in Pakistan where almost every third man is armed . . . with automatic weapons, Kalishnikovs and grenade launchers. What used to be small crimes have now become big crimes, because petty thieves are armed with weapons that can lead to killings if they feel threatened. In 1979, at the advent of the Afghanistan revolution, there were an estimated 110,000 drug addicts in Pakistan, mostly addicted to opium, some to hashish. Today, we have 5 million addicts. Opium has become a big trade through Pakistan. It comes from Afghanistan and Iran. We have an estimated $4 billion trade in Afghan drugs. In a country whose total foreign exports were $6 billion before all this, you introduce $4 billion in trade in drugs. We have created in Pakistan an entire class of rich drug dealers who are paying off this politician here, that bureaucrat there, that port authority there. The political system of the whole country has become enmeshed with the drug mafia. It is not quite as bad as Colombia yet. But it's very close to it.

The third effect is probably the most serious. Pakistan is a very heterogenous society. There are six ethnic groups living together with a combination of antagonism and collaboration. The antagonism consists of something like, "You speak Baluch. I speak Urdu. Our children play together. They have quarreled with each other. My child has beaten your child. . . . We get into an argument over whose child was worse." Previously, it was an argument. Today, bullets can fly. So what used to be, because of ethnic differences in our society, completely minor, local, street arguments, are now made with guns. . . . After a while these little things accumulate and create ethnic warfare.

Are there any progressive political formations in Pakistan?

At this point, no, except in the nonpolitical and informal sector. The primary expressions of progressive formations in Pakistan today are in the media. Since 1987, we have had freedom of the press. It's very lively. In fact, I think I could say without doubt that the Pakistani press today is probably the liveliest in the third world. It's livelier than in India, Egypt, or Indonesia. . . . My articles come out every week. Women are publishing.

The progressive presence is visible in the women's movement. Zia ul-Haq's military regime, which was supported by the United States, was very harsh on women. It passed a number of anti-women ordinances, including the *hudood* ordinances, which reduced women's witness in court cases to half of a man's witness. *Qisas* ordinances ruled that if a woman was murdered by a man, the murder could be compensated for, by paying money. Blood money justifies the murder of a woman.

The first major resistance came from the Women's Action Forum. . . . Ten thousand women came out in the street and the regime took some fright. The police struck them and beat them up. That's when people generally turned against the military. It looked like it must have been a very weak regime to be beating up women. Women have remained very active. Feminism is the most progressive force in Pakistan today.

Various nongovernmental organizations (NGOs) working on the environment, on protection of land, and against large dams supported by the World Bank are having a political impact. But as a political force, progressivism, for the time being, is dormant.

To what extent did Prime Minister Benazir Bhutto contribute to that? She's seen as modern, English-speaking, educated, and progressive. That's the conventional media image.

She was the first Muslim woman prime minister in world history. Educated at Harvard, Radcliffe, and Oxford—where she was elected the president of the Oxford Union, she's articulate. She's an attractive and courageous woman. She fought the military dictatorship after her father was executed by Zia ul-Haq. She went to prison and lived in house arrest. She lived in exile. So she underwent the gamut of political resistance, oppression and suffering.

The people of Pakistan rewarded her by electing her prime minister in 1988. As prime minister she proved to be inexperienced, unsuccessful, confused, directionless, and in some respects misguided. The big bureaucrats, army officers, and vested interests moved against her, and her government fell in 1990. People felt that the vested interests were unjust to her. After all, she was very young. . . . She needed to learn, and they didn't give her enough time.

In 1993, the country elected her again. She made those same mistakes and more. She and her husband, Asif Zardari, turned out to be almost unbelievably corrupt, with bribery, payoffs, bank loans to her supporters, patronage untrammeled. Worse, the corruption was not accompanied by production.

The post-Civil War U.S. government was very corrupt. Former Presidents Ulysses S. Grant and Andrew Johnson could have been indicted, but they were productive. They were capitalist thieves.

What we have learned in Pakistan is that traditional feudal thieves are much worse than capitalist ones. They don't even produce. They create no wealth at all, not even for themselves. They just steal. That's what Ms. Bhutto did.

THE TALIBAN

Moving to Afghanistan and the evolving situation there. The Taliban move-ment, you suggest in an article, has connections with not just Pakistan but also with the United States.

Afghanistan has suffered criminal neglect at the hands of the United States and its media. In 1979 and 1980, when the Afghan people started resisting Soviet intervention, the whole of America and Europe mobi-lized on their side. For the media, it was such a big story that CBS paid money to stage a battle that it could broadcast as an exclusive. Afghanistan was in the news every day. It disappeared from the news the day the Soviets withdrew. Then, Afghanistan was abandoned by the media, by the American government, by American academics, and as a result by the American people. These people who fought the West's bat-tle with the West's money and with the West's arms, and in the process distorted themselves, distorted Pakistan, and contributed to the demise of the Soviet Union, found themselves totally abandoned after the Cold War. The Taliban's rise takes place in that vacuum.

The Afghan *mujahideen* fell to fighting with each other. They were all both warriors and drug smugglers. They were known to the CIA as drug smugglers. . . . There are ten factions shooting at each other, and something new develops. The Soviet Union falls apart. Its constituent republics become independent. Among those are the six Soviet repub-lics of Central Asia: Uzbekistan, Kazakhstan, Turkmenistan, Tajikistan, Kirghizstan, and Azerbaijan. These six Central Asian republics, whose majority population is Muslim, are very close to or bordering on Afghanistan, and also happen to be oil- and gas-rich states. So far their gas and oil has passed through the Soviet Union . . . but now a new game starts: How is this oil and gas going to go out to the world? At this point, American corporations move in.

The American corporations want, obviously, to get hold of the oil and gas. After the Cold War, who controls which resource at whose expense and at what price? Corporations like Texaco, Amoco, and Unocal start going into Central Asia to get hold of these oil and gas fields. But how are they going to get the oil and gas out? . . . Through Turkey and via Afghanistan to Pakistan are two possibilities. Iran is the third, but they don't want to put any pipelines in Iran because Iran is an adversary of America. Therefore, Pakistan and Afghanistan become the places through which they are likely to take pipelines. And then they can cut the Russians out.

President Clinton made personal telephone calls to the presidents of Uzbekistan, Kazakhstan, Tajikistan, and Azerbaijan, urging them to sign pipeline contracts that together amount to billions. These pipelines would go through Turkey and via Afghanistan to Pakistan and take oil to the tankers that would meet them at the ports. The pipeline would go through Afghanistan. Both Pakistan and the United States . . . pick the most murderous, by far the most crazy of Islamic fundamentalist groups, the Taliban, to ensure the safety of the pipelines.

The Taliban are anti-women. Some of the highest U.S. officials have been visiting and talking to them. The general impression in our region is that the United States has been supporting them.

How do you know that high Clinton administration officials have been meeting with the Taliban?

From very insignificant lines in the *New York Times* and *Washington Post*. I have no private information. These are published facts. But they are written in such a way that, unless you are watching very closely, you don't pick it up.

Why would the U.S. support what you describe as the most crazy, most anti-women, most fundamentalist formation in Afghanistan to advance their geopolitical interests? Were not other groups available?

These were deemed the most reliable, perhaps for good reason. In Afghanistan, there are four major ethnic groups. There are the Uzbeks who live in the northern region, near Uzbekistan. There are the Hazaras. They are Persian-speaking, among whom Iran would exercise influence. Therefore, they are not totally reliable. The Tajiks are also Persian-speaking. They have been under Russian influence, but since they are Persian-speaking, Iranian influence on them is potentially strong.

The Taliban come from the Pakhtoon ethnic grouping. They are the majority people. They have a large presence in Pakistan, where we have something like 15 million Pakhtoons. Pakistan has been an old ally of the United States. Its loyalties have been tested. It's much better to have the pipelines under the control of people upon whom the government of Pakistan can exercise some influence, upon whom Iran will have no influence.

The Pakhtoons are Sunnis. The Tajiks are partially Shiias, partially Sunnis. The Hazaras are entirely Shiia. The Uzbeks are Sunnis, but their loyalties are divided. They have never been tested. So there are a lot of ethnic considerations, ethnic politics, and historical ties involved.

The U.S. concern is not who is fundamentalist and who is progressive, who treats women nicely and who treats them badly. That's not the issue. The issue is who is more likely to ensure the safety of the oil resources that the United States or its corporations could control?

One of the leaders of the Afghan resistance against the Soviet occupation was Gulbuddin Hekmatyar. His name has been consistently linked with gun running and drug smuggling. Do you have any information on him?

I met him several times. I don't think he is worse than anyone else. He's a bit more of a killer. He is also more progressive, more modern, much more sensible towards women, for example, than the Taliban.

The Taliban is as retrograde a group as you can find. Their power base is Qandahar, a southern province of Afghanistan. Last year, I spent two weeks there. One day, I heard drums and noises outside the house where I was staying. I rushed out to see what was going on. In this ruined bazaar, destroyed by bombs and fighting from the war, there was a young boy. He couldn't have been more than twelve. His head was shaved. There's a rope around his neck. He is being pulled by that rope in the bazaar. There is a man behind him with a drum. The man slowly beats the drum, dum, dum, dum. The boy is being dragged through the street. I asked, "What has he done?" People said he was caught red-handed. I thought, This is a twelve-year-old kid. What could he have been doing? They said, "He was caught red-handed playing ball." I said, "What kind of ball?" "A tennis ball." "What's wrong with that?" "It's forbidden."

I went off to interview one of the Taliban leaders. He said, "We have forbidden playing ball by boys." I asked why. He said, "Because when boys are playing ball it constitutes undue temptation to men." The same logic that makes them lock up women behind veils and behind walls makes them prevent boys from playing games. It's that kind of madness.

Another time I found the watchman where I was staying literally weeping and very agitated. I asked, "What happened to you?" He said, "They took my radio." I said, "What the hell were you doing? Why did they take your radio?" He said, "I was listening to a singer." Music is banned under the Taliban. People who will ban music and play are, I would say, fifty light years behind the Iranian Islamic regime.

Robin Raphael, the assistant secretary of state for South Asia, an appointee and college friend of Bill Clinton, flew out on a helicopter from Islamabad to meet with the Taliban leaders in Qandahar. So let them not tell me anything about human rights issues in China, of all places. The U.S. government officials lie when they talk about human rights. They're a bunch of hypocrites and liars. You can't take it seriously.

RECONSTRUCTING HEGEMONY

In the 1970s, there was a surge of uprisings and revolutionary activity in Nicaragua, Iran, Angola, Mozambique, and elsewhere. How did the imperial system respond to those upheavals, and how was it able to reconstruct its ideology and its hegemony?

The Vietnam War seems to me to be the most landmark event in modern history since World War II, because it redefined the choices and the strategic design of the United States and its allies.

Between 1945 and 1965, America enjoyed strategic superiority over any power or group of powers, because of its possession and delivery capabilities of nuclear weapons. But by 1968, the Soviet Union had deployed its own intercontinental ballistic missiles and also nuclear submarines. The American nuclear doctrine of massive retaliation had shifted to mutual assured destruction. We had reached a state of madness . . . that greatly reduced the United States' strategic leverage. . . . Europe and Japan had recovered economically. Far from playing the roles of junior partners on the world scene, they were becoming economic competitors. The United States had reduced economic leverage over its allies. . . .

Between 1945 and 1965, the United States demonstrated its power by its will and capacity to intervene in third-world countries in Latin America, the Middle East, Africa, and Asia. . . . So, Jacobo Arbenz doesn't behave in Guatemala? Overthrow Arbenz. The United States and its British allies don't like Mohammed Mossadegh in Iran? Get rid of Mossadegh. Patrice Lumumba in the Congo emerges as a threatening figure? Let's cut him down to size.

In all these cases, intervention worked, and at very small cost to the United States. Henry Kissinger, in 1958, described these as "limited wars." Zbiegniew Brzezinski used to call them "invisible wars"; Huntington called them "forgotten wars," meaning essentially that they were limited in their consequences for the intervening power. They were invisible to the American people. They were forgotten by the American media.

Vietnam changed that. The war that was supposed to be limited in its consequences cost 57,000 lives, 230,000 wounded, nearly $220 billion in expenditure, and thousands of U.S. aircraft. With the anti-war movement and the churches and trade unions screaming, the American establishment understood that it had lost the will, if not the capacity, to intervene militarily in areas abroad.

An additional pillar of American power had been the overriding consensus behind a foreign policy. They lost all of these to varying degrees by 1968.

The U.S. establishment faced the problem of either changing the very course of its policy or finding devices to restore its declining power. The choice it made was that of restoration, not of reconstruction or reform. Restoration means that you adopt a strategy that would bring these four pillars back to their former strengths. As a result, there was this massive and significant shift in strategic weaponry. The United States moved in search of first-strike capability, and second, to lower the threshold on the use of nuclear weapons. These were two prongs of regaining strategic leverage.

The B-1 bombers, the MX missiles, and ultimately Star Wars were all programs aimed at restoring U.S. strategic superiority. In the same way, the introduction of mini-nukes, medium-range cruise missiles, and tactical nukes at the battlefield level were designed to lower the threshold: to say to the Soviet Union, "Look, we can use nuclear weapons in battlefield situations. Don't mess around with us when we intervene somewhere else." But doing this had a sort of a strange and mixed effect. On the one hand, it upped the ante on the arms race. On the other, it frightened a lot of people both in the United States and in Europe, and you had the beginnings of an anti-nuclear movement. Anyway, to gain leverage over allies, American attention shifted from the Atlantic and the Pacific to the Middle East. They assumed that this was an area upon whose oil resources Europe and Japan rely. If the United States could call shots in determining at what price and how much oil will flow, then it would have a powerful leverage over its allies.

In order to develop interventionist capabilities, the Nixon Doctrine was formulated. Its aim was to create regional powers in each significant region of the world, arm them the best you can, and be prepared to support them if necessary. That's why you saw the modernization of the Navy, the formation of the rapid deployment forces, and the creation of the regional allies. Between 1970 and 1978, Iran bought $20 billion in arms, and Israel received $33 billion in grants and aid.

New rhetoric was being continuously found—human rights, a new structure for peace, détente—to justify foreign policy.

Now, briefly, to the economic aspect of it. The structure of capitalism began to change precisely in that period. It went largely, but not entirely, unnoticed by most liberal scholars of international relations. Big multinationals were seeking to leave areas of high labor costs for areas of very low labor costs. They started looking for what multinationals called in those days "export platform countries." There developed a coincidence of export platforms and the regional influential. In Latin America, Brazil, Argentina, and Chile were the regional constellations of American power. They also happened to be, at that time, the countries that were chosen to serve as export platforms for the multinationals. In Asia, Indonesia, South Korea, Malaysia, and to a smaller extent the Philippines were all regional influentials of the Nixon Doctrine. They also happened to be the export platforms of the big multinationals. In the Middle East, Iran and Israel were serving that purpose. Africa was a bit chancy. Nigeria, Zaire, and South Africa were the three that were looked at.

The point I am making is, between the strategic design and the political economy of imperialism there was a coincidence. The second point I am making is that the structure of world capitalism, what is today called globalization, started to develop and change in the 1970s. That process has now matured a little bit more, especially in East Asia. There has been some maturation of it in Latin America. There has been no maturation of it in the Middle East. All that you see in the Middle East is that American power has increased, especially after the Gulf War. The rapid deployment force has now become a permanent presence in the Middle East. The U.S. Navy is now permanently stationed in the Persian Gulf. So while American strategic concentration has become larger in the Middle East, and its military and political power appear consolidated in the region, its economic roots remain weak, because they remain one-sided. The Middle East is essentially a provider of raw material and not an export platform.

A second phenomenon is that discontent remains. The question of Palestine, for example, has been manipulated, but not solved. It may blow up any time. Iraq has been beaten up and suppressed. Five hundred thousand Iraqi children have died for lack of nutrition and medicine. These are not conditions in which you have stabilized power. Iran has been quarantined. How long do you quarantine a country of 60 million people? So American power, while it has greatly expanded in the Middle East, remains extremely vulnerable to local resistances, revolts, and the sheer instability of the situation.

In addition to what you have described, there has also been the imposition on the developing world of what is called neoliberal economic reform, administered primarily through the World Bank and the IMF. These so-called reforms involve shredding the safety net, ending public welfare programs and privatization. Is this part of the restoration of imperial hegemony?

Yes, but the progression of it has been somewhat different. The rhetoric of human rights was greatly prevalent throughout the Carter administration. But the reality was that the regional allies of the United States were mostly tyrannies. Iran and Saudi Arabia in the Middle East. In Southeast Asia, Indonesia and South Korea. They still remain tyrannies. The Philippines of the Marcos period. In Brazil, the military generals. In Argentina, the killing generals. In Chile, Pinochet. These were all fascist regimes committed to the developmental model of export platforms.

Then something happened in 1978 and 1979—most unexpectedly to American policymakers and also to Middle East experts. The Iranian revolution broke out. The analysis that American policymakers made of the Iranian revolution was very interesting. It was that what broke the back of the shah was that he bought too many weapons too soon and his regime was too dictatorial, too authoritarian, and did not allow any mechanism for blowing off steam. It is after the revolution in Iran, beginning in 1980, that you see American policy committed to making very gradual—and they discovered that this is not possible everywhere—progression from developmental fascism to a modicum of political liberalization.

The Philippines, for example. An attempt with Egypt for *infitah*, combining a modicum of political opening with a lot of economic opening. Attempts to help that process in South Korea have not really succeeded. They tried, but the military is so strong there that it has not quite worked. They tried to make gradual change from fascism to some form of liberalized democracy in Indonesia. It hasn't worked. And therefore U.S. policymakers talking about human rights in China look the other way when it comes to Indonesia, which is one of the worst violators on the world scene today. There are several countries that are human rights violators of extreme proportions: Indonesia, South Korea, Israel, and Turkey, and they all remain deeply tied to the United States.

In the Middle East, U.S. policy was to develop strategic assets. Nixon's defense secretary, Melvin Laird, called Israel the "local cop on the beat," taking care of the region.[26] *If that were the case, why did the United States go to such ends and make such efforts to keep Israel out of the Gulf War?*

Israel has been described continuously in this country as a strategic asset. I haven't seen it as serving as a strategic asset. The rhetoric has taken over any sense of reality. . . .

The Israeli military is more war-capable than either the French or the British or even the Chinese, if you're not talking about a long, protracted land war. China, of course, has a large territory and it's a different kind of country altogether. The existence of Israeli power is unquestionably there. What purpose does it serve? During the Gulf War, the greatest challenge for American policy was how to keep Israel out of this war, rather than how to bring it in. The greatest fear American military planners had was that Saddam Hussein might force Israel's entry into the Gulf War. The great fear was, "Oh, my God, I hope the Israelis don't get involved." What kind of strategic asset is that? It makes no sense.

What Israel does do is to keep the area in some respects quite unstable. Just today, I heard that Israeli planes are bombing Lebanon again. On appearances at the moment, the mainstay of American power in the Middle East is not the strength of Israel. It's the weakness of the Arab regimes. In the Middle East today you have armed minorities that are ruling the majorities. The Saudis, the Egyptians, the Jordanians are all armed minorities that are ruling over their people. These are insecure regimes. They are more scared of their own people than of foreign powers. Therefore, they are going to collaborate with the United States and wherever necessary with Israel at any cost. So at the moment American power in the Middle East is based on Arab weakness. How long can that last?

What do you think about the future of Israel?

In the short run, seemingly bright and powerful. In the long run, very dark.

Why do you say that?

The Israeli government, to my total surprise—or not so much surprise, I think we could have expected it—has been missing its chance for the last ten years to make peace with its Arab neighbors. For forty-five years, Israeli officials talked about wanting to be recognized. That was the only basis for peace. Now every Arab government, plus the PLO, openly recognizes Israel's right to exist. They have removed the Arab boycott. Egypt, the largest Arab country, has reached full peace with Israel. The PLO has reached full peace with Israel. King Hussein of Jordan has reached full peace with Israel. But the Israelis are continuing to take Palestinian lands and build settlements.

Their policies are to convince the Arabs that no matter what they are willing to give, Israelis want peace on their terms—more territory and more humiliation of Arabs. More expansion. It can't last that way. Israel is a small country, 5.5 million people. The Arabs are many. They are at the moment weak, disorganized, demoralized, and a bunch of country-sellers are ruling those places. That's not a permanent condition. Someday the Arabs will have to organize themselves. Once they have done that, you will see a different history beginning again, and it won't be a pretty one. In fact, I'm scared of it.

NATO is now seeking to incorporate the former states of the Soviet-influenced Eastern Europe. What are your thoughts on that?

It seems that the president of the United States is committed to the expansion of NATO to include such countries as the Czech Republic, Hungary, Poland, and possibly even Romania. The new secretary of state, Madeleine Albright, is a very strong proponent of NATO's expansion. I think it's correct to assume that U.S. diplomacy is going to push for NATO's expansion hard and fast. What will it do? I think it's very dangerous. It's a dangerous move that could ignite or at least lay down the foundations of another Cold War in a big way. Here is why.

If there is any one thing that moves Russian foreign policy, it is the fear of invasion. Russia has been invaded from Western Europe three times since Napoleon invaded. The last time, when Hitler did it, they lost more than 30 million people. These invasions have all come through the buffer states like Poland and Czechoslovakia. If NATO is expanded there, no matter what rhetoric is used to justify it, no matter how much you mollify Russian fears with words, the fears will be there. Right now, the Russians can't do too much about it. They are weak. They are in disarray. And their power is totally dispersed. . . . But just as I was saying about the Arabs earlier, one day they are going to reorganize themselves. Their weakness cannot be assumed to be permanent.

Every policy that begins on the assumption of keeping someone weak forever is doomed to fail. That was the problem of the Treaty of Versailles. Its primary presumption was—"Give Germany a treaty that will keep it weak forever." Far from it—it gave them deep resentments of a kind that got totally distorted and also had power to give us another war. That's what we are doing with Russia.

Why are they doing it? The expansion of NATO is a mechanism for ensuring continued American power and leverage in Europe. If the Czech Republic, Poland, and Hungary come in, they will be three new members—I'm just taking these three for now—who would support American positions in NATO. And the United States needs more weight to offset France, for example, which is pushing for an independent Europe.

Second, the end of the Cold War has started the search for a new balance of power in Europe. The situation seems to me, both in Europe and globally, very similar to that which followed the defeat of Napoleon at the battlefield of Waterloo and the collapse of Napoleonic France. France and Britain had been competitors for imperial possessions. They fought over possession of India and parts of Southeast Asia. They started competing over portions of Africa. Finally, Napoleon rose to challenge British hegemony on a world scale with the invasion of Egypt. The bipolar world that existed between Britain and France broke down with the collapse of Napoleonic France. What followed was the unchallenged hegemony of Great Britain. From 1815 to 1914, Britain was the paramount power. And the biggest challenge for Britain was to maintain the balance of power between and among the other, smaller powers.

The challenge of balance was of course the greatest in Europe itself. Its overall texture was roughly what it is today. The fear on the part of Britain and France of a powerful Germany emerging to challenge British and French power has been reignited with the reunification of Germany. This time, Germany has reunited with a massive amount of economic muscle. British and French diplomacy are looking to Russia, a reorganized Russia, to balance Germany, and Germany to balance Russia. That is why they would like to deprive Russia of its Eastern European security belt while allowing Russia more influence in the Balkans. One of the reasons Serbia was tolerated in its aggression for as long as it was, and has been rewarded for its aggression with 50 percent of Bosnia, is to ensure that Russian influence in this direction, to Germany's flank, expands, while Russia is cut down on the Czech-Polish front. Without going into great detail, this type of strategic manipulation has been the long-term harbinger of big wars. It was this sort of strategic manipulation that ultimately gave us World War I and finally World War II.

What scholars of Europe call the "long peace," from 1815 to 1914, ended with two world wars. But keep in mind that during this period of long peace an estimated 120 million people were killed in the process of colonial expansion and ensuring the safety of the capitalist market.

Talk about the legacy of colonialism and imperialism today in Africa. We see the fragility of countries such as Rwanda, Burundi, Zaire, and others. These states are imploding.

This is something relatively new, isn't it? We have witnessed in the past six years this extraordinary phenomenon of states simply blowing up through internal implosion. Not revolution. It's not even proper civil war. Somalia was the first, followed by Rwanda. Now we are seeing it happen in Zaire [Congo]. Really interesting questions arise.

The first question is the viability of certain post-colonial states. These states came into being first as administrative boundaries, drawn by colonial powers for the purposes of administration. In the process of decolonization, these became state boundaries recognized under international law. When one transforms administrative boundaries into state boundaries without considering other factors, you will have elements of instability built into it. They don't follow natural lines of any kind, either cultural, geographical, or physical features. So there is an artificiality about a great number of post-colonial states.

There is a second phenomenon that we have to grasp. These decolonizations coincided with the Cold War. The first countries to be decolonized were India and Pakistan in 1947, two years after the start of the Cold War. The last countries to be decolonized were Angola and Mozambique around 1974, at the height of the Cold War. This meant that both superpowers, the Soviet Union and the United States, viewed these decolonized entities as pawns on the chessboard. They were keen to have these. The method of having influence on them was to offer two things: military aid and economic aid. Build their military and bureaucratic structure through the Agency for International Development and the Military Assistance Program and their Soviet equivalents, with the result that these states were maintained by artificial injections of armaments and money. In return, they served a number of purposes, both strategic and economic. They gave economic access. In the process these countries developed great dependency on the metropolitan benefactors. Economic and military aid served as glues to statehood.

The Cold War is over. The structure of aid and militarization disappears. A number of those states which were less important strategically to the United States in the post-Cold War period, and which did not have the patronage of the Soviet Union anymore, started to fall apart.

Somalia is a perfect example. Siad Barre, the dictator of Somalia, was first allied to the Soviet Union. The Soviets put in artificial military and economic muscle into that state. Then aid started to decline with the economic crisis in the Soviet Union. Siad Barre shifted to the United States, which was at the time looking for strategic insertions in the Persian Gulf area. So they took on Siad Barre. More aid flowed in. He stayed on. When the Cold War ended, he was abandoned. The crisis of the state began. It fell apart. The glue was removed.

In 1989, you traveled to the Soviet Union for the first time. Why didn't you go before then?

I had been critical of Soviet communism. I thought it was a rather bad form, a wrong way to run a socialist society. The articles I had written on the subject and the speeches I had given had made me persona non grata with the Soviet apparatchiks. It was not until 1989, when I was a beneficiary of *glasnost* and Moscow University invited me to give a few talks.

That visit made quite an impression on you.

I had, for example, not imagined how unorganic the growth of the Soviet Union had been. A country that produced the most modern research and development in space, jet, laser, and medical technology, did not have a small calculator on the market. There was no organic relationship between one segment of Soviet society and another. I think that the extreme unorganic growth of that state contributed greatly to its collapse. Because with all that military spending, if you have no spin-off into the civilian sector, you're really throwing everything away. Even in America, where there is so much spin-off between military research and development and civilian technology and the civilian market, the country has suffered. There, there was none. It collapsed.

Were you surprised?

I was surprised by the extent of segmentation. I was not surprised that it existed, but really surprised by the extent of it and the demoralizing effect it had on people. The young people at that time, in 1989, really didn't have any belief in the future. It's that loss of faith in the future that must have contributed to the collapse of the state.

The central figure presiding over the demise of the Soviet Union is Mikhail Gorbachev. What is your assessment of him?

It is hard to know if he understood what he was doing. He was a visionary, an intelligent man, but why would he not understand that the process he was introducing was too fast for the system to sustain?

I talked to Alexander N. Yakovlev, who was number two in the political bureau and the person who was seen as the architect of *perestroika* and *glasnost*, a very intelligent man. He studied at Columbia at the time I was at Princeton. He understood that things could fall apart and that they were going in that direction.

As far as the West is concerned, they would have liked China to do the same thing. The Chinese are engaged in very controlled social change. I hope they are able to control it, because the consequences of China falling apart would be very lasting in Asia. It could have a very destabilizing effect. And China is certainly headed towards rocky times. Its rate of growth is so fast that any system would find it hard to contain. In the coastal areas, the Chinese economic annual growth is about 25 percent. Overall in the country it's about 13 percent. It's the highest rate of growth history has recorded. It's booming. You can't take that kind of boom without some strains.

What kind of impact has the collapse of the Soviet Union had on Pakistan?

It has destroyed the dependent communist parties, both Maoist and pro-Moscow, with the result that the comprador left has almost totally evaporated from places like Pakistan, Egypt, and Algeria. I think it's beneficial, because compradorism, dependency of any kind, is not good. Now, the bourgeoisie that controls the state has become more dependent on Washington, the World Bank, and the IMF. The loss of sovereignty is much greater. But at least there is the possibility of the emergence of independent challengers, an independent left.

Segments of the left in the United States, Europe, and elsewhere were very heavily invested politically and emotionally in the Soviet Union. Do you think that was a mistake?

It was a disaster. Not just a mistake. For one thing, it is disastrous in any case for any group or individual to be linked by ties of dependency to anybody, much less a state that was so defective. It renders you uncritical. Soviet communism was one of the most defective formations humanity has seen.

THE FUTURE OF THE U.S. LEFT

What do you see as the future of the left in the United States?

I'm not sure what the future of the left is, but the future of radicalism in America can take non-leftist forms. Jeffersonian liberalism, for example, may have more of a radical future here than the "left" as we have understood it. Some form of anarchism may be more deeply rooted in the American tradition, in which there is a genuine suspicion of government, a genuine objection to the centralization of power. Anarchism may have more of a future than the traditional, orthodox, Marxist left. But I do think that the situation here is not going to remain what it is today. For one thing, the demographic composition of this country is very different from what it was thirty years ago. A very large percentage, probably a quarter, of the total population is now nonwhite, many of them coming from outside the country. This is the first generation of quietists. That's going to change when the second generation grows up to make new demands, to feel fully American, and feel marginalized as they are making new demands.

Secondly, the patterns of inequality are growing. Thirty years ago, I had not imagined that this country would look this unequal or unjust to the lower strata of society. Something like the top 20 percent of Americans earn 45 percent or so of the income. About 4 percent or so control or own 85 to 90 percent of stocks and bonds. These disparities are going to weigh very strongly on people's outlook and lead to anger, especially as they do not see the promise of change.

But is it not in the class interests of the owners and managers of the political economy to provide a modicum of wealth and income for the masses in order to ensure political stability?

That's what the New Deal was about. It was not a socialist form. Franklin D. Roosevelt was one of the finest capitalists around. What he understood was that a modicum of safety, of security, of distributive justice and the stimulation of hope in people is necessary for stability. It is this lesson that the current generation of American rulers is violating. They are going to bring upon this country some sort of an upheaval.

Things are not entirely stagnant and static. You had an experience, for example, in Memphis.

Change occurs, and when it does it happens very fast. When I arrived for the first time as a student, the United States was living in the spell of racism. There were lynchings in the South. When I went to travel with a Japanese and a Brazilian friend to Memphis, for about four hours, from about 4 p.m. to 8 p.m., we couldn't find a hotel that would admit us because we were colored. One was yellow, one was brown, and one was black. We finally found a space in the ghetto. Exactly two years later, we were integrating the lunch counters and hotels. Just ten years later, I would return to Memphis and stay at the Sheraton Hotel. I want to tell you when I got there, I got out of the taxi, and the bellboy who picked up my luggage was white. I was so happy to see that that I tipped him ten dollars, which I could ill afford, when he brought me to my room. After he left, I sat and cried. The change was marvelous. And it took some struggle to bring about that change. We still have a long way to go, but change has occurred.

When the Tonkin Gulf Resolution was passed in 1964 and the Johnson administration escalated the war in Vietnam by starting the bombing of the north, we at the University of Illinois at Urbana-Champaign decided to have a teach-in. This was actually the first teach-in in this country. We arranged for about 150 people in a small hall. We were afraid we would have ten. The place was mobbed. We had to move into another hall. The anti-war movement had taken off. We had no idea it would happen. Social movements are the most unpredictable of historical phenomena.

No one, no scholars have yet found a formula for predicting revolutions or upheavals.

How would you define your own politics?

Socialist and democratic. Those have been my two lasting commitments. By democratic, I mean genuine commitment to equality, freedom of association, critical thought, and the accountability of rulers to citizens. By socialism, I mean control of the wealth by people rather than by the state or by corporations.

You've traveled an extraordinarily long distance in terms of miles as well as intellectually. You grew up in a village in Bihar, India. You migrated to Pakistan. You studied at Princeton. You then worked in revolutionary Algeria. You returned to the United States. You were an activist in the anti-war movement. You had an academic career here. Now you're tying to establish an alternative educational institution in Pakistan. What are your thoughts and reflections on this rather long and varied trip?

What were my choices? Essentially I had two. All my friends from childhood or college days have had to make the same choices. I look at them and in a sense I'm not sorry that I'm not in their position. My choice was to become a regular academic or a corporate executive, to have a very comfortable, boring, selfish, quiet, comfortable existence, as opposed to what I have lived as being very rich spiritually and intellectually and rather poor materially. But look, I have friends from Calcutta to Casablanca, from Algiers to San Francisco. I have the simple satisfaction of knowing that we have tried—we did the best we could and didn't always succeed—but we tried to change where change seemed necessary. I took rather seriously Karl Marx's old dictum that the function of knowledge is to comprehend in order to change.

What do you tell your students?

I don't tell them anything. I think that my life and my teachings all point to two morals: think critically and take risks.

NOTES

1   Jag Parvesh Chander, ed., *Tagore and Gandhi Argue* (Lahore, India: Indian Printing Works, 1945). See also B.K. Ahluwalia, *Tagore and Gandhi: The Tagore-Gandhi Controversy* (New Delhi: Pankaj Publications, 1981).

2   Rabindranath Tagore, *The Home and the World*, trans. Surendranath Tagore (New York: Penguin, 1985). Satyajit Ray, *The Home and the World*, National Film Development Corporation of India, 1984.

3   Larry Collins and Dominique LaPierre, *Freedom at Midnight* (New York: Simon and Schuster, 1975). *Gandhi*, Richard Attenborough dir., Columbia Pictures Corporation, 1982.

4   Stanley Wolpert, *Jinnah of Pakistan* (New York: Oxford University Press, 1984).

5   *Stories My Country Told Me: With Eqbal Ahmad on the Grand Trunk Road*, H.O. Nazareth dir., BBC Arena/Penumbra, 1996.

6   See "Race for a National Anthem," *The Hindu*, December 28, 1998.

7   See Arun P. Elhance, "From War to Water Pacts In Turbulent South Asia," *Christian Science Monitor*, January 15, 1997, p. 19.

8   See Thomas Babington Macaulay, *Selected Writings*, ed. John Clive and Thomas Pinney (Chicago: University of Chicago Press, 1972).

9   Pamela Collett, "A New University for Pakistan," *Chronicle of Higher Education* 40: 34 (April 27, 1994): A35–A36.

10   Frantz Fanon, *The Wretched of the Earth*, trans. Constance Farrington (New York: Grove Press, 1968).

11   Frantz Fanon, *A Dying Colonialism*, trans. Haakon Chevalier, (London: Writers and Readers, 1980).

12   Frantz Fanon, *Black Skin, White Masks*, trans. Charles Lam Markmann (New York: Grove Press, 1968).

13   Frantz Fanon, *Toward the African Revolution: Political Essays*, trans. Haakon Chevalier (New York: Grove Press, 1969).

14   Noam Chomsky, "The Responsibility of Intellectuals," *New York Review of Books*, February 1967. Reprinted in Noam Chomsky, *American Power and the New Mandarins: Historical and Political Essays* (New York: Pantheon, 1969), pp. 323–66.

15   Eqbal Ahmad, "Revolutionary Warfare: How to Tell When the Rebels Have Won," *The Nation*, August 30, 1965, pp. 95–100.

16   Edward W. Said, "The Arab Portrayed," *The Arab-Israeli Confrontation of June 1967: An Arab Perspective*, ed. Ibrahim Abu-Lughod (Evanston: Northwestern University Press, 1970), pp. 1–9.

17   Eqbal Ahmad, "Introduction," in Edward W. Said, *The Pen and the Sword: Conversations with David Barsamian* (Monroe, Maine: Common Courage Press, 1994).

18   Edward W. Said, *The Question of Palestine*, second ed. (New York: Vintage Books, 1992). First edition published in 1979 by Times Books in New York.

19   Edward W. Said, *The Question of Palestine*, pp. 56–114.

20   Edward W. Said, "The Mind of Winter: Reflections on Life in Exile," *Harper's*, September 1984, pp. 49–55.

21   Edward W. Said, *Culture and Imperialism* (New York: Alfred A. Knopf, 1993).

22   Howard Bloom, *The Lucifer Principle: A Scientific Expedition into the Forces of History* (New York: Atlantic Monthly Press, 1995).

23   See Ranajit Guha ed., *A Subaltern Studies Reader, 1986–1995* (Minneapolis: University of Minnesota Press, 1997).

24   See Muhammad Abed al-Jabry, *Arab-Islamic Philosophy: A Contemporary Critique* (Houston: University of Texas Press, 1999).

25   Noam Chomsky and Edward S. Herman, *The Washington Connection and Third World Fascism: The Political Economy of Human Rights, Volume I* (Boston: South End Press, 1979).

26   See Noam Chomsky, *Fateful Triangle: The United States, Israel, and the Palestinians*, revised ed. (Cambridge: South End Press Classics, 1999), p. 535.

PHOTOGRAPHS

Eqbal Ahmad in Boulder, Colorado, with David Barsamian (October 1998). Photo by Urban Hamid.

Eqbal Ahmad in Harrisburg, Pennsylvania (1972). Photo by David L. Morton.

Eqbal Ahmad with Indira Gandhi in Delhi (1979). Photo courtesy of the Estate of Eqbal Ahmad.

Eqbal Ahmad with Yasir Arafat. Photo courtesy of the Estate of Eqbal Ahmad.

Eqbal Ahmad at Hampshire College. Photo by Rebecca A. Kandel.

CHAPTER TWO
DISTORTED HISTORIES

THE PERILS OF NATIONALISM

In March 1998, the Bhartiya Janata Party, the BJP, came to power in India. What are its politics?

First of all, it's anti-minority. It seeks to create out of India—which has for thousands of years been a rather multicultural, multi-religious, and pluralistic society—a kind of uniform *Hindutva*, a Hindu society in the state. Once you have that vision of India, then a number of things follow. They are very resentful of that history of India which is not specifically Hindu from their point of view. That includes the Buddhist part of Indian history. It includes 700 years of what they view as the Muslim part of Indian history, and it includes, to a lesser extent, the colonial part of Indian history. So, one outcome of it is that it is not merely an ahistorical but an anti-historical movement. The BJP's destruction of the sixteenth-century Babari mosque in December 1992 was an expression of that anti-historical outlook.[1]

There is a second aspect to the politics of the BJP: it necessarily turns hostile to minorities. The largest minority in India, of course, are the Muslims, who constitute nearly 15 percent of the population, followed by such groups as Sikhs, Christians, and Buddhists. They all feel fearful that in its drive toward cleansing India of non-Hindu elements, the BJP will commit extreme excesses. Following the destruction of the Babari mosque—which was preceded by a massive mobilization that was quite unprecedented in Indian history and very sectarian in character—there were bloody riots, massacres, and killings of Muslims, particularly in Bombay, in western India, and in Bihar, in eastern India. So this creating a fear, an anti-minority mood, is rather reminiscent; fortunately, it hasn't reached the point—and hopefully will not do so—of the fascist campaign against Jews in Europe or the Serb campaign against Muslims in former Yugoslavia.

The third aspect of the BJP's politics is that this project entails imagining a different history of India. When those in power imagine a different history, they tend to create a different history and certainly destroy an old history. We have seen that with the Zionist movement, which proceeded to create a different history of Palestine and to a certain extent, at least in the Western world, has succeeded in doing so. The racist movements in the nineteenth century proceeded to create a different history, which, for example, ascribed such things as the city of Istanbul to Western creations. Even the Taj Mahal was described as having been built by Italian artists. So, you sort of destroy history and try to create a new kind.

Finally, this will mean, among other things, increasing militarization of India as a country. India has been pulled since the emergence of the colonial encounter in opposing directions of non-violence and violence, of Gandhi and Bal Gangadhar Tilak. It seems that with this movement now in power, a certain, hopefully not a final, ascendency has been achieved by the militaristic wing of Indian nationalism.

In the introduction to the BBC documentary Stories My Country Told Me, *you describe how "all sorts of historical truths and untruths are mixed" by nationalism. When "you organize collective emotion on the basis of difference . . . that's going to promote extremes and hatreds."*[2]

It's happening. I was speaking of nationalist ideologies per se, which generally have those tendencies. Ours was not a great exception. The difference was that there were two different pulls to it, as I just mentioned. The BJP's allies—which are, by the way, much worse than the BJP itself—are pushing it further to extremes. Vishwa Hindu Parishad, Shiv Sena, and most importantly Rashtriya Sevak Sangh, the parent organization of the BJP, are actually fascist organizations. They are pushing this major party, the second largest in India today, to extremes of an ideology of difference. Hindus are different from Muslims. Christians are different from Hindus. Sikhs are different from all. It is producing extremes. Part of that extreme is such excesses as the destruction of a historic mosque or such atrocities as the communal riots that were promoted in various places. Such extremes of militaristic thinking led to the testing of the nuclear bomb for the second time in Pokhran in the Rajastan desert last May. So, a militarization occurs with this ideology of differences. Of course, it could lead to wars and violence, both domestically and abroad.

In the documentary you say, "Nationalism is an ideology of expanded and solidified identity. If you're going to build collective identity on the basis of history, you're going to distort that history."

Not only build collective identity; build collective identity on the basis of the Other. We are so-and-so because we are not the Other. We are what we are because we are different from the West, or from the Muslims, or from the Hindus, or from the Jews, or from the Christians. It necessarily leads to extreme distortions. Examples abound. You see in India today a portrayal of Muslim Mughal rule, for example, in ways that never existed. Historians, for example, pointed out that the majority of the feudal lords and nobility of the Mughal empire were Hindus, not Muslims. They have pointed out that the Muslims of India were by and large a poorer class throughout the 700 years of Muslim rule than the Hindus were. There was more of a propertied class among Hindus. Muslims had mostly converted from the untouchable class to Islam in search of gaining a measure of freedom and equality, since in principle Islam did not have a caste system. But all that is distorted every day.

To their credit, though, I should underline that the large body of the most renowned Indian historians are combating these distortions—just as this new crop of Israeli historians, the so-called revisionists, are now countering the invented history that Zionism superimposed upon the Middle East. The revisionist historians are all Jewish. They are doing a most commendable job of providing a corrective to the distortions of nationalist ideology.[3] This was actually not done in the same way in the more intense period of European fascism. The revisionist doctrines against European fascism eventually occurred from its opposition and in the postwar period rather than internally from within itself. What is interesting about India, Pakistan, and Israel is that the distortions of nationalism are being recognized now by a new generation of historians who are offering corrective interpretations.

It would seem in the case of those three societies that they're deeply divided. There is much internal dissension.

A very great deal. This is especially true, less reported, of India and Pakistan, than it is of Israel, but it's true definitively of Israel. Edward

Said has been impressed very much, and I think his outlook on the Israeli-Palestinian conflict has slightly shifted, since his last two visits to Israel.[4] He has seen at the tip of Israeli intellectual life signs of a recognition that Zionist ideology created deep distortions of outlook, of comprehensions of history, about the understanding and attitudes toward the future and toward the past. And that this has to be given up, corrected, if we are going to live like normal people. This new wave of ideologists, such as BJP chauvinists in India, right-wing Zionists in Israel, and Muslim nationalists in Pakistan—one can multiply examples—have actually done deep damage to their own people by robbing them of their real history. These are cases, in a sense, of theft, of robbery, of suppression that should not have been tolerated. But the truth is that there are critics of these distorted histories all over. How much impact they will have, we don't know; hopefully they will have an impact in the long run.

Even here, in the United States, Noam Chomsky's voice is frankly suppressed by the institutions of power, including the media. He is one of the premier intellectuals, if not the premier one. There is also Edward Said. They are not being published in the American press. They are not the ones who appear as pundits on American television. Yet, wherever they speak, they draw large crowds of young people. Their books are being read. One hopes that they are not merely cult figures, but that they are speaking to the future.

SOME OF THE NEWS FIT TO PRINT

You used to write fairly frequently for the New York Times. *It's been literally years since you had an op-ed in the paper. What happened there?*

It is rather ironic, I think, that the *New York Times* was publishing me quite frequently during 1978 to 1980, when A.M. Rosenthal, a right-wing Zionist, was its editor.[5] The ban on us, including Edward Said, has occurred generally speaking from the time that Joseph Lelyveld, a very liberal Zionist, came in as editor. I am suggesting, then, that a change of personnel might have had something to do with it. Because Rosenthal was a right-wing Zionist, he probably felt that he would be freer from attacks of bias if he used a few tokens like myself or Said.

There is a second reason, I think, a larger one. There has been a very deep shift in the climate of this country toward the right. It is this change that defines this extraordinary phenomenon that a twice-elected American president from the Democratic Party has been the one to effectively abolish the gains of the New Deal and is yet by and large applauded despite all his dissimulations, lies, and undignified behavior. What is remarkable is that the liberal Democratic establishment, including the media, have mostly been favorable to Clinton. Two days after admitting that he had committed perjury and had lied about having sexual relations with a twenty-one-year-old in the Oval Office, he launches a military attack on Afghanistan and Sudan without giving reasonable proof of anything. He engages in an untrammeled unilateralism, and the newspapers, including the *New York Times*, come out editorially to say that he is now acting like the commander-in-chief of the United States.[6] There has been a shift in this environment toward intolerance of dissent, toward defining once again the boundaries of dissent, which had been broken during the Vietnam War and the civil rights movement. It's the breaking of those boundaries by young people that allowed us to become visible in the mainstream. Those boundaries have been redrawn, and we are on the other side of it. That's the larger question than the personnel issue of Rosenthal and Lelyveld.

Lastly, intellect as a whole is under assault in America, and social intellect in particular. The scientist can do whatever he wants to. But the social intellect is under assault in very insidious ways. The publishers are not really publishing radical works. The media are extraordinarily full of vacuous talk. People sit around on television and radio talk shows and pontificate on Islam, China, Japan, India, the Arabs. None of them that I can recall knows a single language of these places on which they are pontificating, can identify five central dates of our history, can look at the roots of any struggle. We happen to be talking at a time when Osama bin Laden is a central figure of the news and discourse in America. To date, no one has examined what has produced Osama bin Laden. There have been hints that he worked with the CIA, that he first engaged in violence because he was brought in to fight the Soviet Union in Afghanistan. There are hints that he was recruited into the *jihad* by the CIA. The United States and the Saudis financed it. But this is not enough. No one has identified how his country, Saudi Arabia, has been robbed by Western corporations and Western powers. No one has identified what bin Laden grew up seeing. The Saudi princes, this one-family state, have handed over the oil resources of the Arab people to the West and its investment firms. He has seen it being robbed. All through this time, he had only one satisfaction: his country is not occupied. There are no American, French, or British troops in his country. Then he realizes, in the early 1990s, that even this small pleasure has been taken away from him. He has already been socialized by the CIA, armed by the Americans, and trained to believe deeply that when a foreigner comes into your land, you become violent. You fight. That was what the *jihad* in Afghanistan was about.

This whole phenomenon of *jihad* as an international armed struggle never existed in the last five centuries. It was brought into being and pan-Islamized by the American effort.[7]

TRIBES HAVE BEEN GIVEN FLAGS

There were so many things in your answer that lead into many different areas. Let me just take one thread and cite Robert Fisk in The Independent. *He writes about "the growing fury of thousands of Saudis," about the "continued American military and political presence in the land which is home to Islam's two holiest shrines, Mecca and Medina. It was not by chance that the bombs that exploded in Kenya and Tanzania in the U.S. embassies occurred on the eighth anniversary to the very day of the arrival of U.S. troops in Saudi Arabia following Iraq's invasion of Kuwait in 1990. U.S. forces were invited into the kingdom by the now-ailing King Fahd, who insisted that the Americans withdraw all their military forces once the threat of Iraqi aggression had ended. The Americans did not keep their promise, and today thousands of U.S. military personnel are still based in Saudi Arabia, with key operatives inside the Saudi ministries of defense and interior, just as they were in Iran before the fall of the shah."[8] So, he's making a comparison between Iran and the shah in the 1970s, which looked like an impregnable U.S. ally, a fortress, and Saudi Arabia in the 1990s. Is that a credible parallel?*

More than credible. In the early 1980s, a fairly senior CIA official who had either retired already or was on the brink of retiring wrote a very interesting article in the *Armed Forces Journal.* The article was entitled "The American Threat to Saudi Arabia." What's interesting about this long article was that a CIA analyst wrote under the name of Abdul Qasim Mansoor. He took an Arab name to hide his identity. His argument primarily was that the policies that the U.S. government and corporations were pursuing out of greed were going to turn Saudi Arabia into another Iran, a totally dependent state and one extremely vulnerable to revolution. Osama bin Laden is a sign of things to come. The United States has no reason to stay in Saudi Arabia except exploitation and greed. Saudi Arabia is not threatened with invasion by anyone that we know of. Any potential aggressor, such as Saddam Hussein, has already been knocked out.

Moreover, the Americans demonstrated in 1991 that they are capable of mobilizing against any attack on an ally in the Middle East. What, then, is the justification of an American military and intelligence presence in Saudi Arabia? Every ministry is infiltrated with American advisers. It is creating deep discontent there. The answer is money. Money in ten different ways. Saudi oil is essentially controlled and marketed by American interests. Saudi wealth is invested in the United States and Europe. The Saudis went into the arms market early in the 1980s. The United States has dumped something like 100 billion dollars' worth of armaments in that place. The Saudi people are going to be discontented. Fisk is totally right.

I want to add something else. Saudi discontent shouldn't be seen only as Saudi. Unlike Iran, Saudi Arabia is an Arab country and is part of the Arab world. Therefore, the discontents that occur in it are also occurring around it. The Arabs are at the moment an extremely humiliated, frustrated, beaten, and insulted people. They are the guardians of our Muslim holy places, and they have not been able to guard them. They are the only people who since the creation of the United Nations have lost territory to invaders and not been able to regain it. Syria remains an occupied country. Lebanon remains partly occupied. Palestine has been totally occupied, and its people continue to lose land, water, and lives. In this situation, they make agreements with the United States supervising. Those agreements are not honored. They sign accords. The accords are not honored. They are violated night and day, as Oslo has been. The United States promised redresses and doesn't do anything. The Arabs have only two choices now, as its young people see it. It's either to become active, fight, die, and recover its lost dignity—lost sovereignties, lost lands—or become slaves.

If you look at the situation from the standpoint of the Arabs as a whole, this is a most beleaguered mass of 200 million people. They have a wealth of oil, and that wealth is not reaching them. Their oil wells have been separated from their people. Tribes have been given flags: Kuwait, Abu Dhabi, Saudi Arabia. The Saudi tribe has been given a state in order to separate that oil from the people. These are issues that the media should at least have looked into. They don't have to agree with this analysis, but they must look into the history of a conflict. Terrorism is not without a history. All social phenomena have historical roots. Nobody here is looking into the historical roots of terror.

I'm wondering how you can lump all Arabs together. This is a very diverse mosaic of peoples and cultures.

Arabs have a few things in common. One is language. We know that language is a strong link. The second is history. They have a very common history over time. Third is, most important, identity. They have a common identity. Obviously the Saudi family or the Kuwaiti sheiks, do not feel any identity with their poor Arab brethren. But the Arabs as a whole have a certain sense of identity. I'm only talking in those identity terms.

If you look at the question of identity, America is a very diverse country. There are black people here, Mexicans, white people, new immigrants. All somehow, within a fairly short period of time, acquire a thing called American identity. So that when America invades someplace, they somehow identify with the president, for better or for worse. The Arabs at least identify when they are invaded; they at least have the identity of being victims. What is actually uniting them at the moment is a sense of common loss, common humiliation.

NUCLEAR POLITICS IN SOUTH ASIA

Let's get back to events in South Asia. What triggered India's decision to set off underground nuclear explosions in mid-May 1998?

It did not make sense for a number of reasons. Rationally speaking, it made no sense whatsoever for India to have tested its nuclear weapons a second time, and made equally no sense for Pakistan to follow suit. Therefore, the only way you can explain India's decision is this particular brand of Hindu nationalism the BJP represents. The BJP's notion of power is military power. It believes influence is attained by force or the show of force. I am not sure that considerations of Pakistan played any role at all in their decision to test nuclear weapons. I think they were testing to become equals of the other nuclear powers. They tested in the expectation of joining this silly abstraction called the *nuclear club*. The privileges of this membership are not clear to me or to anyone. If it is clear to somebody, nobody has explained it to me.

I think it was this notion of nationhood as powerful and power as being linked to military prowess. Otherwise, it made no sense. After nearly thirty years of failure to improve relations with China following the India-China war of 1962, India's relations with China were improving rapidly. All India's and China's neighbors were starting to think that closer and friendlier ties between the two great giants of Asia would be to the benefit of all third-world people. Last year, the Chinese president and prime minister visited India and Pakistan. In Pakistan, they urged the Pakistani leadership to make peace with India, even if it meant making compromises on Kashmir. This was the greatest single achievement of Indian foreign policy in the last ten years. In a single day, the BJP leadership destroyed this achievement and turned China once again into an adversary. The nuclear explosion test in Pokhran was preceded by a huge amount of anti-China rhetoric. India cannot afford an arms race with China. It will be disastrous for India, just as Pakistan cannot afford an arms race with India.

Secondly, India has been a surprising country economically. In the forty years after decolonization, its economic growth had hovered around 3.5 to 4 percent. Despite the fact that it's a country with massive resources, both human and material, its growth rate remained very low. Economists couldn't figure out how to explain it. As social scientists do, when they can't find a real explanation for something, they invent a phrase. So, they started calling it the "Hindu rate of growth," as if there were something cultural about it. Then, in the last seven years, India broke out of the Hindu rate of growth and its development curve started going up. In 1997, India's growth was 7.5 percent. In 1998, it was projected to be 7 percent, but the nuclear testing has brought India's rate back to 4 percent. Why did they hurt themselves? What India needs most at the moment is to feed its poor, of whom nearly half, 400 million people, are living below the poverty level. They do not have the required amount of caloric intake to survive as healthy people. Why did they come back to the economic cycle they had been caught in earlier?

Thirdly, India has ambitions to be a regional power. One basic principle for a regional power is that it should have better relations with its neighbors. The previous government of Inder Kumar Gujral had been successful in improving relations with Bangladesh, Sri Lanka, and Nepal. By exploding this bomb, India once again has increased tension in this region and frightened its smaller neighbors. If there is a nuclear war in South Asia, it isn't only Indians and Pakistanis who will die. South Asia is an ecological unit. In this ecologically unified unit, a bomb would hit everybody, because the wind blows every which way and distances are short.

Prem Shankar Jha, a columnist for The Hindu, *an Indian daily, lays the blame for India's action on Pakistan's doorstep. Writing in May 1998, Jha commented, "India went ahead with its test only after Pakistan changed the power equation on the subcontinent by launching its intermediate-range ballistic missile, the Ghauri, on April 6. At the time Pakistani spokesmen said that with the development of the Ghauri, brazenly named for the Afghan invader [Shahabuddin Ghauri] who established the first Muslim kingdom in north India in 1193, no Indian city was safe from a Pakistani attack. Then a few days later Pakistan announced that it would soon test a longer-range missile named the Ghaznavi, for the first Afghan to invade western India in search of plunder at the end of the tenth century. The aggressive intent behind the naming of the missiles and the harping on the ability to hit Indian cities sent shivers of apprehension through India," thus, according to Jha, provoking the Indian response.[9] What do you think of that analysis?*

First of all, as a Pakistani, I should say that the testing of the Ghauri was a mistake. It was not necessary. The naming of this missile, which had previously been called Hatif, is outrageously crass, crude, and in some ways provocative. It is also totally ignorant. The naming of the Ghauri was based on the total linguistic ignorance of the Pakistani government and its officials. Before Ghauri, India had already deployed along the Pakistani border a missile system called Prithvi. The Indian leaders had already made similarly provocative statements that Prem Shankar Jha quotes Pakistanis as having made, and I condemned them. There's no justification for either of the two sets of statements.

"*Prithvi*" means "earth" in Hindi. The Pakistani rulers didn't know that. They thought Prithvi was named after Prithvi Raj Chauhan, who was the twelfth-century Hindu Rajput king who had defeated Shahabuddin Ghauri several times. He was finally defeated by Ghauri. So, they were thinking that the Indians had named it after Prithvi Raj Chauhan. They decided to name their missile Ghauri. What it illustrates is that we are dealing with medieval minds, with distorted histories. Prithvi Raj Chauhan was not fighting Shahabuddin Ghauri because he was a Hindu. Shahabuddin Ghauri was not fighting Prithvi Raj Chauhan because he was a Muslim. These were medieval rulers, conquerors, invaders, invader in one case and king in the other, who were fighting for land, territoriality. In case Prem Shankar Jha does not know, Shahabuddin Ghauri did not fight Prithvi Raj Chauhan until after he had defeated half a dozen Muslim rulers who came in his way. But what is happening, what we were talking about earlier, is what's coming back to us. Distorted histories have created a new kind of medieval history: "Hindu history" and "Muslim history." These distorted ways of looking at it created these two misunderstandings, Prithvi on the one hand, Ghauri on the other.

We should recall that a missile race was on when the Pakistanis tested the Ghauri. An Indian missile system called Prithvi was already deployed everywhere. And the more advanced Indian missile system named Agni was already tested before the Ghauri. So, for Prem Shankar Jha, who is supposedly an independent journalist, to come out and ply nationalist lines is not useful. I think we should begin by recognizing that Pakistani and Indian rulers are caught in medieval militaristic minds. They are no more modern than the Clintons and the Bushes, who see power in terms of military prowess. We are living in modern times throughout the world and yet are dominated by medieval minds.

Prime Minister Nawaz Sharif, after the May explosions, said essentially that Pakistan had no choice. It had to even the playing field. Do you think Pakistan had a choice?

Of course it did. From the evidence that was before us, it seems clear that after testing their weapons, the Indian leaders became panicky that they would look very bad if Pakistan did not test. They made the kind of provocations just after testing that Prem Shankar Jha is accusing the Pakistani government of doing after the testing of the Ghauri. The Indian foreign minister said Pakistan should reconsider its position in South Asia because the strategic equation had changed. L.K. Advani, the home minister, said that India was going into Pakistan to take over those parts of Kashmir that were in Pakistani hands. Atal Behari Vajpayee, the prime minister, said that the strategic equation had changed and the Pakistanis should understand it. These kinds of provocative statements were made every day. Some fighting also started along the border in Kashmir.

However, to respond to such provocation is not the act of responsible leadership. I would be as wrong as Prem Shankar Jha if I argued that Pakistan had no choice but to explode its own weapons. What fields needed to be evened? I argued then that there was no need for us to test. I'm arguing now there was no need for a test. Just because India had done it and Indian leaders had made provocative statements does not mean that one should be provoked. . . . I don't believe in nuclear weapons. Therefore, I believe that just because India has nuclear weapons, Pakistan does not have to have them. I believe in unilaterally not having to compete with India in the nuclear arms race.

In the New York Times *report of the events following the Pakistani explosions, John Burns wrote, "Within hours, Prime Minister Nawaz Sharif declared his country a 'nuclear power,' fulfilling a secret plan made by a predecessor nearly thirty years ago that Pakistan would build an 'Islamic bomb.'"* [10] *What predecessor is he talking about?*

He's talking about Zulfikar Ali Bhutto, who never said "an Islamic bomb." This is a misquotation that began about twenty years ago and has continued to spread. Zulfikar Ali Bhutto made a lot of mistakes and committed a lot of excesses, but he did not say that he was going to build an Islamic bomb. What he reportedly said, is that everybody has a bomb. The Jewish people have a bomb. The Christian powers have a bomb. Now India, seeing itself as a Hindu power, is developing a bomb. Why shouldn't Muslims also develop their own bomb? He came close to talking about an Islamic bomb, but that's not exactly the phrase he used.

I doubt that the Pakistani bomb is Islamic. I argued very strongly in Pakistan that it wasn't. Among other things, it has not been circumcised. Secondly, Pakistan is like any other nation-state. Unfortunately, this bomb has to do with Pakistan and not with Islam. It has to do with Pakistan's fears of and competition with India and not with anything else. If India had not tested its bomb in 1974, Pakistanis probably would never have started to develop their bomb. I do not defend such competition. I do not defend either responding to provocation. I think these are all childish acts, not acts of national security.

What is at the root of what's been described by Akbar Ahmed in his book Jinnah, Pakistan, and Islamic Identity *as a deep sense of insecurity among Pakistanis?* [11] *I saw pictures of demonstrators in the streets after the explosions of Pakistan's nuclear weapons with signs stating, "We're willing to eat nothing but grass and sticks, but we'll have an atomic bomb."*

First of all, the Pakistanis' sense of insecurity is there. But I want to first of all clarify two things. There were expressions of joy at the testing, both in India and in Pakistan. In this respect, the Pakistanis were not very different from the Indians. Second, it was a microscopic minority that expressed joy in both countries. In the case of Pakistan, I am a witness to the fact that most of the pictures that appeared on television in the first three days after the May 29 test were the result of the hunger of Western media for photo opportunities. I saw exactly what happened. The day after the Pakistani explosion, the world media descended on us. In the morning, officials held a press conference for these media people. There is an area in Islamabad called Apara. Government agents went there and told shopkeepers to close their shops and to come out to show their support for the bomb. Probably a maximum of fifty or sixty people gathered. They were handed bouquets of flowers. Two officials went into a *halwai*, a sweets shop. They bought a whole lot of sweets and started distributing them. Then they instructed the camera people to take pictures. That was the demonstration in Islamabad. I did not see any expressions of spontaneous joy either in Islamabad or in Rawalpindi.

A week later, Nawaz Sharif went to Lahore. There his Muslim League Party organized a mass demonstration to welcome him and therefore the bomb. This was all official. These were state-sponsored events which the Western media did not recognize as entirely staged. Whether or not the same thing happened in India, I do not know, but I wouldn't be surprised if exactly the same thing happened there.

The Indian public and the Pakistani public, even those who felt joy about it, know that this was too serious a matter to go about celebrating. This was not a moment of celebration. In both countries, large demonstrations took place on Hiroshima Day this year. In India, the demonstrations have been much larger than in Pakistan. In Calcutta, 250,000 people came out against nuclear weapons. In Delhi, 30,000. In the Western world, no such demonstrations took place within the first two years, or even the first ten years, of the bombing of Hiroshima and Nagasaki. I'm not saying this to condemn the West, but to say that the consciousness of the risks, the dangers of nuclear weapons, is much greater today than it was in 1948 or 1950.

But back to Pakistani insecurity. The country feels insecure for a number of reasons. I think most important is that the country has emerged from a partition of India. Many of the issues linked to that partition have not yet been resolved. Kashmir is one of them. Therefore, it is this sense of insecurity that India has not quite accepted the fact of Pakistan's existence. The Pakistanis are wrong. In my view, India, including the Hindu nationalists, has accepted the fact of partition.

Secondly, the country already broke up once, when Bangladesh was created. East Pakistan seceded from Pakistan, arousing a sense that maybe things are not final yet. Lastly, a sense of stability hasn't developed. Out of the last fifty years since partition, twenty-five have been spent under military rule and twenty-five under unstable, corrupt, and inefficient civilian rule. People who have been living in that unstable fashion, facing a very large, hostile neighbor, created out of historic India, therefore not certain whether their status is permanent or not, will feel insecure. That's another reason I feel we should have avoided the possession of nuclear weapons.

But the genie is out of the bottle. It's not going to get back in.

Therefore all the more reason that the international community has a responsibility to put pressure to keep the genie in the bottle. There is international pressure on Pakistan and India. There is no international pressure on Israel to keep the nuclear genie inside the bottle, to not make a bigger and bigger bottle, and to not make it more deliverable. So, the question really is the refinement of the genie and the refinement of the delivery capabilities. You can't put the genie in the bottle, but you can arrest its growth.

NATIONALISM AND ISLAM

What about the state and condition, both materially as well as psychologically, of India's vast Muslim population? Few people know that, after Indonesia, India has the largest Muslim population in the world. What about their sense of belonging, particularly in this atmosphere of communalism?

It's an interesting question. I think the Indian Muslim identity was very much shaken by the partition of India in 1947. It was deeply shaken because many of them sympathized with Pakistan and its creation. Many of them became confused about what partition means and who they are. Surprisingly, fifty years later, and this may be a great achievement of Nehru and Gandhi's secular ideals, the Indian Muslim feels quite Indian—insecure on grounds of being a Muslim, especially because of the rise of these Hindu fundamentalists, but Indian, not alien, not different, not an outsider, not somebody who should think of going away somewhere. There's a saying in Urdu that translates roughly as "Here is where we will receive our rewards and punishment. This is where we will be until the day of judgement." They have a sense of Indianness. When I went back for the BBC documentary, I sensed that much more. It's very different from the Arabs in Israel and the occupied territories. They don't feel Israeli. They don't feel they have been taken into the state, that they belong to it. The Indian Muslim feels that he's Indian, and he's going to bloody well stand up and fight for it. That's an important achievement of the Indian National Congress and the leadership of Gandhi and Nehru, I think, which people are not willing to recognize. It's an important achievement also of that Muslim leadership which has stayed in India, which opposed the idea of Pakistan, people like Abdul Kalam Azad.

But that leadership also included teachers and Muslim clerics.

It included all the Islamic scholars, the *ulema*, of India and Pakistan. In fact, by and large, the *ulema* did not support the Pakistan movement. Ironic, but it's true. Just as the greatest Judaic scholars in the 1920s and 1930s did not support the Zionist movement. They thought it was inimical to the notion of Judaism, to the universal idea of being a Jew.

But today in Pakistan the Muslim fundamentalist parties are decidedly nationalist, wouldn't you say?

I don't think they can be called "nationalist." They are decidedly Islamist. They are out to capture state power. In that sense they are nationalist; however, they are not quite nationalists in the sense that we use the word. They are pan-Islamists.

They wish to establish a theocratic state?

They wish to establish a theocratic state in Pakistan as the first step toward theocratic states elsewhere. They are part of a generalized theocratic movement in the Muslim world today, which was given a massive push and an armed character by the efforts of the United States in Afghanistan. What happened in Afghanistan has not been discussed in the West. When the Soviet Union intervened in Afghanistan, the U.S. saw in it an opportunity that was twofold. One, they hoped to tie up the Soviet Union in a Vietnam-like war in Afghanistan itself. Two, which becomes more important later on, they saw an opportunity to mobilize the entire Muslim world in a violent way against the Soviet Union, against communism. In an effort to mobilize the entire Muslim world against the "evil empire," the CIA started supporting the flow of volunteers from all around the world to fight in Afghanistan, to be socialized into the ideology of anti-communism, and to be trained to hit communists wherever they found them. That's how the militants were recruited and flown in. I have seen planeloads of them arriving from Algeria, Sudan, Saudi Arabia, Egypt, Jordan, even from Palestine, where at that time Israel was supporting Hamas against Al Fatah, Yasir Arafat's faction of the PLO. These people were brought in, given an ideology, and told that armed struggle is virtuous—and the whole notion of *jihad* as an international, pan-Islamic terrorist movement was born. The U.S. has spent billions in producing the bin Ladens of our time. In 1986, I visited the camp they hit in Zhwahar, Afghanistan, in 1998. It was a CIA-sponsored camp. Even after the Soviets withdrew from Afghanistan, the United States did not withdraw its support from bin Laden and others. They continued their support.

The Soviet Union collapses in 1990. From 1991, you see a new phenomenon. The United States broke faith with a lot of these people. Promises that were made were broken. Help that was being given was withdrawn. Worse, the United States first moved in on the issue of drugs. Afghanistan and Pakistan had become the largest centers of the drug trade in the 1980s. Many of these people who were supported by the CIA were also engaged in the drug trade. Now the United States did not need them. So it started pressuring the government of Pakistan and the government of Saudi Arabia to clamp down on these groups that were previously working with the United States. They suffered from a double betrayal. There was a failure to continue to fulfill promises made, and there was a turning on old friends.

Who are these people? The majority are tribal. Osama bin Laden comes from the bin Laden clan. Ramzi Yousef is an Afghan-trained fellow. Aimal Kansi is a Baluch tribal.

Ramzi Yousef was identified with the World Trade Center bombing.

Aimal Kansi has been convicted of killing two CIA agents. Bin Laden is the Saudi millionaire who is alleged to be behind the United States embassy bombings in Kenya and Tanzania in 1998. Ramzi Yousef is of uncertain origin, probably a Pakistani. He grew up in Oman and then came to fight in Afghanistan. But they are all Afghanistan-connected, CIA-connected people. They are also tribal people with a code. Two words are central to that code: "loyalty" and "revenge." The tribal system works around the notion of loyalty and revenge. When your friend to whom you are loyal has betrayed you, you will take revenge. These people have enough of a grudge now on the basis of having been loyal and having been betrayed, number one. Number two, they have been socialized, trained, and equipped to carry on a war of terror against foreign occupiers, which was the Soviet Union in Afghanistan. Now when they see their lands occupied by the United States, as bin Laden does, it raises a different issue. Bin Laden is merely carrying out the mission to which he committed earlier. Now he is carrying it out against America, because America, from his point of view, is occupying his land.

UNILATERALISM AFTER THE COLD WAR

The U.S. missile attack on Sudan and Afghanistan is eerily reminiscent of attacks on other countries over the last few decades in this ongoing war against terrorism. There's the now-familiar routine and rhetoric, the high administration officials and generals with their maps, pointers, and satellite photos of the targets. The cast of characters keeps changing but there seems to be something constant among Abu Nidal, Muammar Qadaffi, Saddam Hussein, the PLO, and now bin Laden. They are the incarnation of evil and demons which must be exorcized.

That's understandable, isn't it? The pattern repeats itself continuously. The real questions are really: what is it doing to the world, to the United States? What kind of international system is emerging from it? All the images that you have just described are associated with the Cold War. The Cold War is over, but the phenomenon continues. Interventions go on. What does it mean? What does it mean in terms of political culture in the United States? What does it mean in terms of the insecurities that relatively weaker nations feel in our time? What does it mean for international institutions such as the United Nations and the U.N. Charter? What does it mean for such institutions as the International Court of Justice?

What is remarkable in this period is that the United States is acting unilaterally and declaring its right to act unilaterally when it is the superpower that has access, in some cases controlling access, to international institutions. Why did it not go to the court in Rome and present to it the evidence, on a secret basis if they so wished, that it had against the camp in Afghanistan and against bin Laden and his connection to the factory in Khartoum? There is a fundamental principle of politics, which is that when power has no countervailing forces balancing and checking it, it is always abused. It's abused in extreme ways. The most dangerous characteristic of the current period is that a single power dominates the world militarily and dominates international institutions of peacekeeping and law without countervailing forces. That makes the current world system much more dangerous, especially for the weak and the poor, than even during the Cold War. We are in a time much worse than the Cold War.

You're not suggesting that the prospect of nuclear annihilation which was present in the Cold War is similar to the current situation.

The prospect of nuclear holocaust has probably been marginally reduced, only in the sense that the threat of the Soviet Union and the United States blowing each other up is not there. But the threat of nuclear war in all other areas remains. Nuclear weapons remain. The possibility of misuse of those weapons remains. The possibility of accidents remains. Miscalculations remain. Proliferation remains. There is now no balancing mechanism in the uses and misuses of power. All modern systems of government have been built on the notion that checks and balances are essential to the responsible exercise of power. At the moment, in the international system, there are no checks, no balances, formal or informal, and that makes it more dangerous.

THE LEXICON OF TERRORISM

Dawn, *the English-language newspaper in Pakistan that you write a weekly column for, discussed this very issue of unilateral action in a unipolar world, writing in an August 23, 1998, editorial, "Who will define the parameters of terrorism, or decide where terrorists lurk? Why, none other than the United States, which from the rooftops of the world sets out its claim to be sheriff, judge and hangman, all at one and the same time."*[12]

That's exactly true. Because in a different way than what I was saying earlier, it totally violates the current international system. It stands against the fundamental principle of justice. It's a single power that claims to be judge, accuser, and executioner. You don't allow that in your system. We don't allow it in our system. But we are allowing it on a world scale. Take the case of the missile attack. There is increasing evidence now that the pharmaceutical factory which was hit in Khartoum, Sudan, was not producing any chemical weapons or any weapons of mass destruction. The U.S. government claimed that its intelligence says that it was. But if there is anything that distinguishes the intelligence of the United States, or any other country, it is the number of times they are wrong. A British manager who worked at the factory until last year says there is nothing that could possibly be used for weapons. A foreign cameraman who has filmed the factory says nothing could be seen.[13]

You wrote an article some years ago called "Comprehending Terror" in which you said it's important to start by defining the terminology.[14]

First of all, I think terrorism should be defined in terms of the illegal use of violence for the purposes of influencing somebody's behavior, inflicting punishment, or taking revenge. If we define terror in that way, the first thing we discover is that it has been practiced on a larger scale, globally, both by governments and by private groups. Private groups fall into various categories. The political terrorist is only one category out of many others. When we talk about terror, then, we are talking about the political variety. When we talk about the political variety, the first thing to ask is, what are its roots? Who is the terrorist?

The official attitude toward terror suffers from a suspension of any inquiry into causation. We seldom ask what produces terrorism. There is no connection, said Secretary of State George Shultz, with any cause. Terrorism is just a bad crime. Official definitions, even academic definitions of terror, exclude the illegal violence: torture, burning of villages, destruction of entire peoples, genocide, as outside of the definition of terror, which is to say the bias of terror is against people and in favor of governments. The reality is that the ratio of human losses between official and terrorist activity has been one to a thousand. For every life lost by unofficial terrorism, a thousand have been lost by the official variety.

Another characteristic that we have seen of terror in our time, if you take my definition of it, is that there was a rise of fascist governments in third-world countries, particularly throughout the 1970s and 1980s. All these fascist governments—in Indonesia, Zaire, Iran, South Korea, and elsewhere—were fully supported by one or the other of the superpowers. They have committed a huge amount of terrorist violence, the source of which is the state. Again, there has been very little focus on this by governments, the media, and even academics.

Religious zealotry has been a major source of terror. Terrorist activity is associated almost solely with Islamic groupings. No focus is given to terrorist activities of other religious groupings. It's a global problem.

Jewish terrorists have been terrorizing an entire people in the Middle East, with the support of the government of Israel, which is supported by the government of the United States. That terror has included killing people, destroying homes and shooting children, including shooting worshipers in a mosque. The latter happened in Hebron. There's very little focus on terrorism of other religions like Judaism, or for that matter, Hinduism. These people have committed murders and massacres after massacres. They have committed crimes against humanity in the name of religion. Again, our focus, our attention, is uni-focal, on the Islamic variety, not on the Christian, Jewish, Hindu, or Buddhist variety. In other words, it's a parcelized approach to terror.

Modern terrorism has a whole lot of phenomena attached to itself. Regarding the political private terrorists, on whom all the attention at the moment lies, there is a lot of condemnation, a great deal of narrative about what they have done, a great deal of denunciations and government investigations and bombings and counterterror, but very little inquiry as to what they are about. If I had to identify a few factors explaining the roots of terrorism, I would say first of all the desire to be heard. Palestinians, for example, introduced hijacking. This was their innovation, in a sense, during the late 1960s and early 1970s. Nobody was listening to them for more than thirty years. They had been completely deprived of their land, their country, and nobody was listening. They shook the world up by hijacking airplanes. That kind of terror is a violent way of expressing long-felt grievances. It makes the world hear you. It's normally undertaken by small, helpless groupings that feel powerless. The Vietnamese never committed terror. The Algerians did not commit terror of this kind.

Secondly, terrorism is an expression of anger, of feeling helpless, angry, alone. You feel like you have to hit back. Wrong has been done to you, so you do it. During the hijacking of the TWA jet in Beirut, Judy Brown of Belmar, New Jersey, said that she kept hearing them yell, "New Jersey, New Jersey." What did they have in mind? She thought that they were going after her. Later on it turned out that the terrorists were referring to the U.S. battleship *New Jersey*, which had heavily shelled the Lebanese civilian population in 1983.[15]

Another factor is a sense of betrayal, which is connected to that tribal ethic of revenge. It comes into the picture in the case of people like bin Laden. Here is a man who was an ally of the United States, who saw

America as a friend; then he sees his country being occupied by the United States and feels betrayal. Whether there is a sense of right and wrong is not what I'm saying. I'm describing what's behind this kind of extreme violence.

Sometimes it's the fact that you have experienced violence at other people's hands. Victims of violent abuse often become violent people. The only time when Jews produced terrorists in organized fashion was during and after the Holocaust. It is rather remarkable that Jewish terrorists hit largely innocent people or U.N. peacemakers like Count Bernadotte of Sweden, whose country had a better record on the Holocaust. The men of Irgun, the Stern Gang, and the Hagannah terrorist groups came in the wake of the Holocaust. The experience of victimhood itself produces a violent reaction.

In modern times, with modern technology and means of communications, the targets have been globalized. Therefore, globalization of violence is an aspect of what we call globalization of the economy and culture in the world as a whole. We can't expect everything else to be globalized and violence not to be. We do have visible targets. Airplane hijacking is something new because international travel is relatively new, too. Everybody now is in your gunsight. Therefore the globe is within the gunsight. That has globalized terror.

Finally, the absence of revolutionary ideology has been central to the spread of terror in our time. One of the points in the big debate between Marxism and anarchism in the nineteenth century was the use of terror. The Marxists argued that the true revolutionary does not assassinate. You do not solve social problems by individual acts of violence. Social problems require social and political mobilization, and thus wars of liberation are to be distinguished from terrorist organizations. The revolutionaries didn't reject violence, but they rejected terror as a viable tactic of revolution. That revolutionary ideology has gone out at the moment. In the 1980s and 1990s, revolutionary ideology receded, giving in to the globalized individual. I've spoken in very general terms, but these are among the many forces that are behind modern terrorism.

During the period of the embassy bombings in East Africa and the U.S. attack on Sudan and Afghanistan, the media reported that terrorist formations have "mutated." Whereas before, as you suggest, organizations like the PLO, the Red Brigades in Germany, the Basque-separatist ETA in Spain, and the IRA were much more politically driven, today it's religious-driven groups—therefore more irrational and, by extension, more dangerous.

I am not sure that they are necessarily more irrational. You will allow me a certain dissenting voice on the left from the left also. One of my biggest problems early, it started in 1968, with the PLO was that I kept arguing with them that the violence they were practicing was a violence of the oppressed, but it was not revolutionary violence. It fundamentally lacked the content of revolutionary violence. It had no mobilizing content to it. It was just not morally or politically rooted. It was psychologically and sociologically not selective. It was more an expression of a feeling than an expression of a program. Quite frankly, I feel now that after twenty-five years of being critical toward them, my point of view has been upheld by history. The PLO was not a revolutionary organization. It was an organization of the oppressed, carrying on nonrevolutionary tactics with a non-revolutionary program by a nonrevolutionary organization. The same is true of the Red Brigades.

The IRA is a different fish. It has swum in a different sea. That's why it has lasted as long as it has and that's why it brought the United States and Britain to the negotiation table, which the PLO did not. The PLO went to surrender. The most tragic point about the PLO is that Israel has not accepted its surrender.

Thomas Friedman of the New York Times *said that the terrorists "are driven by a generalized hatred of the U.S."*[16] *Is that enough to drive these kinds of operations?*

Thomas Friedman is a *New York Times* columnist. One does not associate either intelligence or depth with a *New York Times* columnist. Thomas Friedman writes without information or knowledge. It's an ignorant remark. It's a waste of time to try to respond to it. He actually in that article said that they hate America because America is so wealthy. He said that they hate America because it has technology and science and their children are all imitating America. This is nonsense. This is not analysis. This is witchcraft.

David Anderson is a senior lecturer at the School of Oriental and African Studies in London. He comments that this battle will be a "long, perhaps never-ending, attritional war. Pandora's box has been opened, and it won't be closed again," discussing this issue of retaliation, counter-retaliation, an eye for an eye.[17]

I don't see anything as historically permanent. Nothing in history has been permanent. Frankly, I don't think American power is permanent. It itself is very temporary, and therefore its excesses are impermanent and reactions to those excesses have to be, by definition, impermanent. If Anderson means the next five years, then he's right. If he means the next fifty, he may not be right. America is a troubled country, for too many reasons. One is that its economic capabilities do not harmonize with its military capabilities. The second is that its ruling class's will to dominate is not quite shared by its people's will to dominate.

What's the evidence for that?

The evidence is massive. If the American people had a will to dominate the world, they would have lynched Bill Clinton at the first sign of his hanky-panky in the White House. I'll tell you why. Britain had a will to dominate in the eighteenth and nineteenth centuries. Britain punished for very small crimes its most famous empire builders. Robert Clive was impeached and Warren Hastings was impeached, because an imperial society instinctively knows that it will not command respect on a global scale unless it shows uprightness at home. Unless it shows uprightness at home, it cannot commit excesses abroad. That's why imperial countries very often tended to be puritanical societies. The people of America don't want Clinton to resign because they think he's been a good president. They can separate his being commander-in-chief from his personal behavior. This is not a people with a will to rule. This is a people with a will to violence, yes, but not a will to dominate.

You can take other examples. A will to dominate means a willingness to sacrifice, to pay the price of it. The American public does not want American boys dying. So, in Somalia, when American Marines were attacked, the United States pulled out and sent in Pakistanis to do their dirty work and clean up the mess. They don't want to send troops abroad. They don't want to die in foreign lands. That is, they don't want to pay the price of power abroad, which they were willing to do during much of the Cold War. This changes after Vietnam. In that sense, George Bush notwithstanding, the "Vietnam syndrome" is very much alive.

ENGAGING IRAN

Iran now has someone who is considered a "moderate" president, Mohammad Khatami. There have been some openings between the United States and

Iran. What's your assessment of what's going on now inside Iran itself politically and externally? Does this signal a possible normalization of relations with the United States?

There has not been any opening between the United States and Iran yet. There have been gestures. The American wrestlers went there and the Iranian wrestlers came here and that kind of thing, but there has been no substantive opening between the two countries. Mohammad Khatami's government is being challenged by the radical conservatives in Iran. Therefore, what you are witnessing in Iran today is a struggle for power between two brands of Islamic politics. It's Islamism in both cases. One is more democratic than the other. One is more moderate, the other more radical. One has been in power, the other has not.

Khatami is new. He comes in with new social forces behind him. It is a very interesting struggle because beneath it are very fundamental issues about the future of Iran or the future of any third-world, particularly Muslim, society. Issues of the nature of the relationship between civil society and the state. Issues of the nature of culture and the relationship of culture to power. The issue of the nature of power itself: how is it to be made more accountable to the citizen, to the public? What is the nature of public discourse, the nature of the relationship between faith and politics? Those are all very fundamental issues at stake in the current struggle for power in Iran.

Khatami's group, if we are to use Western terminology, and it is not always applicable, represents an enlightened liberal view of the relationship between power and civil society. This group would like to see women freer, with fewer constraints than have been imposed on them under the present Islamic rule. They would have more freedom of speech and association than was allowed by the revolutionary system under Ayatollah Khomeini or than would be allowed by the conservative groups. They would seek more normal relations with Western countries and with America than the previous leadership. For all those issues, even in terms of the overall expression of Iran's politics, this is progress over what had preceded Khatami's administration. But remember that this government is the product of an election. Iran has continued to hold free elections, with fewer choices, but still free elections, which is not true of Saudi Arabia.

One would think that the Islamic theocracy in Iran would be sympathetic and supportive of a neighboring theocracy in Afghanistan, the government of the Taliban. But that's not the case at all. Iran is actively supporting what is called the "northern alliance" under Ahmed Shah Masood. What's going on there?

There is nothing surprising there. For one thing, we should not see Islamic movements as monolithic. There is a large variety of them. They range from the very modern to the totally primitive—in fact, so primitive that in the whole of Islamic history there is no parallel to them. The Taliban, for example, are literally unique in Islamic history in many respects. They are a product of modern times, of a certain social disease. The immediate reason for Iran to feel antipathy to the Taliban is that they are viewed by Iranians as suffering from two terminal defects. The first is that the Taliban were supported by the United States.

Initially.

Until recently, actually. They will again be supported by them once this Osama bin Laden issue disappears. The second is that they are sectarian, orthodox Sunni Muslims. The Iranians are Shiites. As sectarian Sunni Muslims, they hate Shiites. It's like fundamentalist Catholics up against fundamentalist Protestants, both trying to set up a theocracy. Obviously there will be conflict between the two. It's a bad analogy, but it comes closest to what I can cite to you.

Recently there have been a number of advertisements and articles from U.S. commercial interests questioning the policy of sanctions and isolation of Iran. Particularly the U.S.-dominated oil, gas, and chemical multinationals are lobbying the government to reconsider its position. What do you make of this particular situation, where it seems that ideology is trumping commercial interests? Usually the commercial interests dominate, but here several U.S. administrations have seen it more important to isolate Iran diplomatically and to pay whatever economic cost that incurs.

It's an interesting problem. This is one of the myths of the left. Sometimes noncommercial vested interests get the better of commercial vested interests. A very good example would be the China lobby in the 1940s and 1950s. They were primarily responsible for blocking the United States from opening up to China—which the United States has done now, but almost twenty-five years too late—despite the fact that it was not in the American interest to maintain the blockade on China.

Something similar is happening in the case of Cuba, especially after the fall of the Soviet Union. A lot of American companies are interested in getting into Cuba. It's ninety miles away from the American coast. It has nearly 95 percent literacy, a skilled labor force, and an educated middle class. It would make a very good export platform because it also has very cheap labor; yet it remains closed because of the Cuban lobby. The lobby is very powerful. It bribes Congressmen. It has political action committees. So, it's a case of the tail wagging the dog.

The same is true of Iran. The Israeli government still doesn't approve of Iran. It feels that Iran is a big Middle Eastern country not wanting to accept Israel's control of Jerusalem. Therefore, Israel says Iran is dangerous and must be isolated. I think the Israeli lobby has done a lot to keep Iran isolated.

The New York Times *had a front-page story on Iran testing a medium-range missile with a range of 800 miles. The headline says it is able to hit Israel and Saudi Arabia.*[18] *They could have mentioned Turkey, Pakistan, or Afghanistan. Why the choices?*

Because Israel is a strategic ally and Saudi Arabia has a strategic position. By saying that, you are creating a public opinion. The American public doesn't care if Iran hits or doesn't hit Pakistan. It cares if it hits Israel or Saudi Arabia, although it has less reason to hit Saudi Arabia and Israel than it has to hit Pakistan. It's not about to make war on either.

Let's go back to that idea you expressed about commercial interests vs. non-commercial ones. For example, in Guatemala, the United Fruit Company had an enormous economic interest there, and it was able to influence the 1954 coup.

I didn't say it's always the case. Occasionally it is the case. The norm is that commercial interests get their way. Their pressure groups are very strong. But occasionally you'll get a situation in which a very strong pressure group forms and creates for itself a cultural legitimacy. A convergence occurs between the rhetoric of the state and the pressure group. Take Cuba, for example. Cuba has been portrayed for almost forty years as a bad boy in the rhetoric of American officialdom. The media have by and large supported that. A lobby has developed along with that. It's incredibly strong in some ways. It's very focused. It has only one goal:

to prevent the resumption of normal relations between Cuba and the United States.

TURKEY AND ISRAEL

What are your views about recent events in Turkey? There seems to be a struggle between some Islamicist formations and more secular ones.

It has been nearly eighty years now since Turkey declared itself to be European. Turkey's identity has developed for the last eighty years away from the Middle East. Its ruling class doesn't want to be part of the Middle East. Turkey therefore has found itself making an alliance with Israel. On the other hand, the people generally know that they are not really Europeans, after all, and recognize that even more now. You have an Islamic movement that has taken hold in Turkey. It's a strong movement; in fact, it was the party in power and was dismissed unconstitutionally by the intervention of the army. Turkey is a troubled country because it is falling between the Middle Eastern stool and the European stool, and it doesn't seem to fit the crack.

What's the logic behind Turkey's military alliance with Israel?

The logic of that is that Turkey has at this moment one major ally and benefactor: the United States. The U.S. has helped forge the alliance between Turkey and Israel. The logic is really to encircle the Arabs. The Arabs are at the moment, if I could use the term, the true captive peoples. At the same time, they are a people who are showing signs of not wanting to remain captive. Therefore, the United States fears that they may rise again or they may learn to resist. When they resist, the U.S. will need a strong policeman to put them down. Israel and Turkey are very good allies.

THE ARMENIAN GENOCIDE

The genocide of the Armenians in 1915 by the Ottoman Turks is called the first genocide of the twentieth century. Turkish governments continue to deny it to this day.

You may disagree with me on this one because I don't think it was done by the Ottoman Turks. The Turkish genocide of Armenians was the first expression of Turkish nationalism. The caliphate was still there, the Ottomans were still ruling, but they were already ceasing to be Ottoman rulers and becoming Turkish nationalists, which is why they lost the Middle East. They lost the loyalties of the Arabs because they turned to nationalism. Armenians had lived with the caliphate in relative safety until this particular ideology of difference, that is, nationalism, took hold. The ideology was that anyone who was not a Turk by blood was the Other. The Armenians were not killed for being Christian. They were killed for being Armenian. The Armenians in a very genuine sense were the first victims of the rise of nationalism in the Middle East. The Jews were the last victims of the rise of nationalism in Europe. And I hope that the Kurds are the last victims of the rise of nationalism in the Middle East.

Princeton University has now a chair funded by the Turkish government on Turkish history. Its principal function is to refute the genocide of the Armenians.

Is that really true? My God. All I can say, in that case, is that it's one more thing that Princeton is doing that I'm ashamed of. I think that the Turkish people will not be a free people until such time as it comes to terms with its own history, especially its modern history, which includes the genocide of the Armenians. To say that it was a civil war is like saying that Turks were not a majority people. It is also like saying that Turks were not the upholders of power. Power was in their hands; a majority was in their hands; and the territory was theirs. They cannot dismiss it all as a civil war. They will be a bigger, greater people if they acknowledge this, just as I think the Germans are a bigger people today because they acknowledged the Holocaust. The Israelis would be a bigger people today if they acknowledged that they have committed a crime, a massive crime, against the Palestinians. The same is true of the Turks with the Armenians.

What you're suggesting is something that makes some Israelis very uncomfortable, the symmetry you were outlining there, the genocide of the Armenians, the Holocaust, and the Israeli treatment of the Palestinians.

It has been the destruction of a people. I should have added the Americans with American Indians. It's my failure that I did not remember the American Indians. But all that the Americans can say, if they want to say it in their favor, is that they didn't do it all at one time in a specified time and space frame. All that the Israelis can say is that they didn't really build gas chambers. For God's sake. They took lands from people; they took away water; they destroyed a culture. They are still doing it. A people doesn't survive if you take away from them their land, water, and culture. They drove people away. This is what the Israelis did in Palestine. True, the bloodshed was not the same; the number of heads chopped off was not the same; the number of deaths was not the same. Yet deprivation of a homeland, an attempt to obliterate a people from their soil, was there. Unfortunately, this is still going on. So, yes, I know how much the comparison must grate on the Israelis, and perhaps also on the Armenians. In fact, I found it striking that the Armenians I met in the Middle East, particularly in Palestine and Lebanon, were so strongly pro-Palestinian precisely because they knew instinctively that there was not symmetry, that these four cases are not symmetrical. They may be asymmetrical, but they are on the same terrain. One is a higher peak than the other, but the terrain is the same.

Your views on Zionism are largely I think shaped by your earlier comments on opposition to exclusivity and "the pitfalls of national consciousness."[19]

I praised earlier the Indian nationalism of Mahatma Gandhi and Jawaharlal Nehru, because it was not exclusionary. It did not envisage a Hindu India in which there was no space for Muslims or Christians. In Israel today, even today, after the majority of the Palestinians have been either driven out or expelled—or are remaining as an occupied people—those Palestinians who are given citizenship rights are still third-class citizens. They don't have full citizenship rights. You speak to any American Jew here and ask him if he would like to live in America under the conditions that the Arab lives in Israel. His answer would be no. Don't say I'm making a comparison with Israel, because then his answer may change. Say, "Supposing as a Jew your property could be taken over by the state for security reasons while the same thing can't happen to the Christians." Say, "As a Jew you cannot join the armed forces, but the Christians can. Therefore, as a Jew you will not have access to the housing, to the educational scholarships, to the welfare system, to those lands to which Christians have access. Would you call yourself a citizen of America?" His answer would be no. It's an exclusionist state, a racialist state. I'm sorry.

BEYOND BELIEF: V.S. NAIPAUL

V.S. Naipaul was born of Indian ancestry in Trinidad in 1932 and emigrated to England in 1950, where he has lived since. He's a much-heralded novelist.

Two of his novels were recently listed among the "100 Best" of the century.[20] *He has been knighted. He also writes non-fiction. In 1981, he wrote* Among the Believers: An Islamic Journey, *which according to his publisher received universal acclaim.*[21] *In 1995, Naipaul traveled to Indonesia, Iran, Pakistan, and Malaysia. His latest book,* Beyond Belief: Islamic Excursions Among the Converted Peoples, *is his account of those travels. In his prologue, Naipaul says,*

> *Islam is in its origins an Arab religion. Everyone not an Arab who is a Muslim is a convert. Islam is not simply a matter of conscience or private belief. It makes imperial demands. A convert's worldview alters. His holy places are in Arab lands; his sacred language is Arabic. His idea of history alters. He rejects his own; he becomes, whether he likes it or not, a part of the Arab story. The convert has to turn away from everything that is his. The disturbance for societies is immense, and even after a thousand years can remain unresolved; the turning away has to be done again and again. People develop fantasies about who and what they are; and in the Islam of the converted countries there is an element of neurosis and nihilism. These countries can be easily set on the boil.*[22]

What is your take on Naipaul's assessment?

I think you have put your finger on the problem by quoting at some length the introductory paragraph of *Beyond Belief.* The central thesis is that Islam in the countries he visited is Islam of converted people. He calls Islam "an Arab religion." Everyone who is not an Arab is a convert to Islam. A convert's view is distorted and nihilistic. It produces disturbances; it's a condition of neurosis. So, the central thesis rests on the impact of conversion on the converted. Throughout this book, Naipaul identifies a problem in Pakistan or in Malaysia and says it exists because the people were converts to Islam. At one point, for example, he describes quite correctly how some of the greatest historical monuments in one of the oldest cities in Pakistan, Lahore, have been criminally neglected. He describes the neglect and he asks how can a people allow Versailles-like structures to be so neglected? Clearly it is because these people have no relationship to their history. Converts don't care about the past. That's his conclusion. But it's an unfortunate fact that historical monuments are being neglected in India, Pakistan, Cambodia, Egypt, Jordan, Africa, Latin America, and all over the world. They're even neglected in many European countries and in America. What does that have to do with converts? There's that problem. His central thesis is wrong.

There is a second problem that is even greater. Who is not a convert? By the definition he is giving, if Iranians are converted Muslims and Americans are converted Christians, the Japanese and large numbers of Chinese are converted Buddhists. Everybody is converted because every great religious system has had only a few followers at the beginning. Given that, Christianity, Islam, Buddhism, Judaism, especially all the prophetic religions, developed through conversion and have produced an entirely distorted humanity. In that sense, his organizing thesis should not exclude anyone. You are wasting time.

V.S. Naipaul is a man haunted by imagined, created ghosts. None of his ghosts are actually real. They haunt him in very unexpected ways. In this book, for example, it's about Islam. But suddenly, in the chapter on Pakistan, he spends the major portion of it on a particular person whom I'll discuss in a moment, a character he calls Shabaz. Here is a British-educated young Pakistani who discovers Karl Marx, V.I. Lenin, and, above all, Che Guevara while studying at Oxford and Cambridge. He returns home and—like young people of that generation in Latin America, Africa, the Middle East, or America—he joins a leftist group and ultimately a leftist armed uprising in Baluchistan. Naipaul goes into very great detail of this person's narrative. He makes him look like some sort of a distortion. At the moment, I'm not debating with you or telling you whether this person is a distortion or not. But that's how Shabaz looks as he goes through this rigamarole of a leftist uprising that doesn't work. His friends die and he goes back to normal life.

Nowhere is there any suggestion in this entire chapter that Shabaz was a believing Muslim, that Islam had any role in his life, his education, or his thinking, or had any role in the narrative on which Naipaul is spending thirty-five pages. He comes in for only one reason. Shabaz appears because Naipaul is haunted by his hatred of everything leftist. He finds an opportunity to discover his ghost. As soon as he discovers his ghost, whether it fits his narrative or not, he vomits out his fears, hatred, and disgust.

There is another aspect to this, which is rather typical of this type of Orientalist, racist scholarship. That is, Naipual cannibalizes his friends. The Shabaz of his book is a man who is my friend, Ahmed Rashid. He took Naipaul as a personal guest during his six-week visit to Pakistan, showed him around, and introduced him to a myriad of people, including me. Ahmed was generous to a fault. He dropped a lot of other things he was doing to help Naipaul in his work. Naipaul has repaid him by writing a caricature. He changed his name but only in such a way that every educated Pakistani would recognize Ahmed Rashid in that book and will pity him for having befriended this cannibal of a man.

Naipaul is, and it doesn't please me to say so, a very sick man. This book is actually beyond belief, perhaps because it's a book driven by ghosts. Islam is one of his ghosts. He's like Captain Ahab.

Islam is his white whale?

Islam is his white whale, and he's really after it. The only difference is Ahab at least had a good reason to go after the whale, the whale had hurt him. To the best of my knowledge, Naipaul has never been hurt by Muslims or Islam. Yet he is obsessed.

What was your encounter like with Naipaul? How did he engage you?

He didn't engage me. I met him several times. . . . The initiative was his, but he didn't engage me. I was wondering why. I think, one, I didn't look like somebody who was going to give him a subject to write about. Two, he asked me what I thought of his book *Among the Believers* and I said I disliked it. He said, "Why?" I said, "Because you are not interested in reality. Books like these are not fiction. I read books like these for reality." He became very agitated. He said, "What do you mean, I'm not interested in reality? That's what I write about." I said, "You wrote nearly sixty pages on Pakistan in *Among the Believers*. You are describing there Pakistan as an Islamic state under Zia ul-Haq, the military dictator who had created a halcyonic Islamic government. You are describing it throughout as if this government represented that country and was supported by its people. It was your responsibility to at least report, mention, that the regime was being opposed at great risk to themselves by hundreds of thousands of people, including almost all the known poets, writers, and artists of Pakistan. Our best writers of that time were in prison or in exile. Numerous people had been flogged in public. Nearly 30,000 or 40,000 went into prisons, and you don't make one mention of it. You describe that regime as Islamic. The least you could have done was to say that this was a contested space. This Islam that you are presenting is not the final Islam of Muslims. It is contested by a large number, most probably a majority, of the Muslim people of Pakistan." He disliked hearing that.

It is really rather scandalous. Faiz Ahmed Faiz, the greatest Urdu poet since Iqbal, was living in exile. Habib Jalib, another outstanding poet, was in prison. And in the sixty pages, a serious writer coming from London would describe the regime of Zia ul-Haq and the society he was creating without mentioning that we were all suffering in prisons or exile. This is not writing. He should stop writing. He should be selling sausages.

THE CHANGING OF THE GUARDS

You write about "the tenacity with which colonial culture has, after decolonization, held out and tightened its grip on Pakistan and India as a case in point. Its persistence is defined by the failure of the post-colonial elite to spawn alternative values and styles as foundations of a new culture."[23]

The post-colonial state is a bad version of the colonial one. The structures of the post-colonial state are the same, that is, a centralized power, a paternalistic bureaucracy, and an alliance of the military and landed notables. The structure of the state has remained the same; but new problems have emerged, and this old system cannot work. . . .

The colonial state was not about being of service to the colonized. It was about exploitation and extraction of resources. The post-colonial state is exactly the same. This intelligentsia, this bourgeoisie—the propertied class of the third world—is as heartless in its lack of concern for the poor, in some ways even more so, as the colonial state. There has been a near breakdown of the institutions of higher learning. A new intelligentsia, rooted in that soil, informed of the country's problems, having some sense of responsibility as to what is happening to people, has not been produced. They are now sending their children to American universities, just like Iranians did a bit earlier. There were 60,000 Iranian students studying in the United States at the time of the Iranian revolution in 1979. There are 15,000 to 20,000 Pakistanis studying here now. More will be coming. Even the middle class, the intelligentsia, is cut off from the problems of the people. They are building a system of apartheid in which the poor are separated from the rich and the rich are connected to the West, to the metropolis. It's a bad situation. I hope it will change. I should not give you as bleak a picture, because there are people who are trying to turn this tide in a different direction or stop it; they are small, but they are trying.

Yeats wrote about something you're describing in his poem "The Great Day": "The beggars have changed places but the lash goes on." So, even with independence, there hasn't been significant change. Didn't Frantz Fanon say liberation is not merely changing one policeman for another?[24]

I don't remember the exact quote, but that was roughly his argument also: unless we think in terms of alternatives that empower people and make alternative plans for economic growth, then the future remains quite bleak. Fifty years after the start of decolonialization, I think we are turning around to admit that it was a necessary step but not a sufficient one. We have not gone from the necessary to the sufficient.

Groups like the Third World Network, based in Penang, Malaysia, suggest that through the mechanisms of so-called free trade agreements, the International Monetary Fund, and the World Bank, the hegemonic powers have to some extent recolonized the former colonies.

I agree with the argument, but I have one difficulty with it. It seems to me that we are always reinventing the wheel in which we have been caught anyway for a long, long time. I don't think that we are going through a process of recolonization because we never really went through the process of decolonialization. Take my country. Pakistan is a large country; it has a population of 140 million now. The British ruled this area with the help of three institutions: the army, the bureaucracy, and the feudal landlords. The army and the bureaucracy had top commanders who were English. Top civil servants were often English. Just below them there were a large number of Indians serving them. See the structure. The reality was that our economy was tied to the metropolitan economy. We produced to supply Britain. We bought our consumer goods mostly from Europe or the industrialized world.

Now take a look at Pakistan for the last fifty years. It's exactly that situation. A British-trained army, a British-trained bureaucracy, and the same feudal landlords who had collaborated with the British constitute the triangle of power. We buy most of our armaments from the West and China. We produce very little on our own. Most of our big products come from industrialized countries. The numbers have increased. Previously imports came from Britain. Now it is mostly America, plus Japan and Germany. Globalization has increased the number of buyers and sellers in our countries. Nothing else has changed. So, the economic reality has not changed and the political reality has not changed. Why, then, should we talk about recolonization? Pakistan never became a *de*colonized country. Never. And it is not being recolonized in the period of globalization. Globalization is merely changing the structure of the international economy. It is not changing the structure of our economies.

The Indian environmentalist and activist Vandana Shiva told me a story. She went to a village and was describing globalization, the expansion of multinational corporations into India and elsewhere. A villager wasn't quite getting it. Then all of a sudden he said, "Oh, now I understand. The East India Company has returned."

That's a very good story. The Company Bahadur, they used to call them.

The East India Company being perhaps the first of the multinationals.

There was the Dutch East India Company and several others. The East India Company was the ultimate winner in India. Today, of course, the intensity and scope of multinationals have increased vastly. The means of communication and production have increased. The rapidity of production and the power and capabilities to reproduce have expanded enormously. With increasing volume, the number of traders and producers has increased. But the structure has not changed. I'm afraid that I'm more conventional in this regard. I go with the *Monthly Review* group's argument that the structure of capitalism has not changed significantly. Its intensity and scope have.

RETURN TO THE SOURCE

What were the circumstances of the BBC documentary on you?

The BBC originally said they wanted to do a profile and they wanted to do a longer thing on nationalism, with Bishop Desmond Tutu, Eric Hobsbawm, Maxine Hong Kingston, and me. They wanted to tell a story of our time through the lives of individuals. . . . I agreed to be part of the project. As the film was produced and they saw the overall takes, they decided that Hobsbawm's segment and mine should also become separate profiles with additional materials. So, that's what you have seen. It was interesting because it created a structure for me to return to my village in Bihar, which I hadn't seen since partition.

Has PBS, which is the BBC equivalent in the United States, shown the documentary?

PBS is very strange. The BBC did a very successful film on Edward Said and his work, *The Idea of Empire*, and they did this documentary on me.[25] They are both American documentaries in some ways. Both of us have lived here and made some name here, Edward of course much more than me. We have played a role in American history: I in the civil rights and anti-Vietnam War movements, and other things, and Edward in the academy particularly. Yet PBS and no other American network has ever thought of replaying them. A lot of money has been spent in doing these documentaries by the BBC. PBS takes things like *Masterpiece Theatre* from the BBC but nothing serious like this.

In the film, you travel along the Grand Trunk Road. What was your idea behind selecting this big highway?

I lived along it. It was very simple. The Grand Trunk Road was built in the sixteenth century by the Emperor Sher Shah. It ran from Calcutta to Peshawar. For me it symbolized the unity of India. Then the two nationalisms, Indian and Pakistani, broke up the Grand Trunk Road. It lost its continuity only in 1947. It is rather strange that you suddenly come to a particular point in India where the Grand Trunk Road stops. Then you pass the Pakistani and Indian checkpoints and the Grand Trunk Road resumes.

I also had a childhood association with it in multiple ways. I lived around it, grew up around it, traveled on it throughout my childhood, and then romanticized it from reading Rudyard Kipling. You remember that Kipling, a colonial writer but a good writer nevertheless, wrote a lot about the road. So, I thought that the road would be the defining symbol of both the unity and the breakup of the subcontinent, and of my life.

You return to your village, Irki, which you last saw when you were thirteen or so. It's a very happy scene. All the kids are around you. You are like a returning celebrity. You recall many things. For example, you say that you remember the tradition of two communities living side by side and you mention that after Id prayers your Hindu neighbors would come and congratulate the Muslims.

Id is a Muslim festival that comes at the end of Ramadan, the month of fasting. On that last day of fasting, Muslims all go to a mosque and pray. When they come out, the festivities begin, people visit you, and are offered sweets. There were two mosques in my village. Id prayers were in one mosque, not the other. Right outside the mosque, all our Hindu friends came to congratulate us and wish us well.

The first thing I saw as I was approaching the village for the film was the mosque. I recognized the village from the mosque. It was also very touching to see how much the villagers, both Hindus and Muslims, fifty years later, had remembered, loved, and revered my family. As the word passed, they kept coming to see me. The older people were particularly touching because they remembered and asked about particular individuals. But it's a poorer village than when I left. We had a great library. My grandfather had built a library of nearly 5,000 books, which included about 3,000 manuscripts. All of it was destroyed during the killings and riotings of 1946 and 1947.

So Irki was not spared from communal violence?

Irki saw some communal violence. Not much, but some. Others suffered much more.

There's a poignant scene where you visit the village graveyard and comment on a particular irony that gave you both pleasure and pain.

My father's tomb has disappeared. Just across the graveyard, you see some peasant homes that are built of bricks and stones taken from the graveyard. It was very painful, but also a pleasure to see the dead giving life to the living, making their lives better. It's much better to use those stones in a home than in a tomb. It's fine. I think my father would have been happy.

The film starts in Calcutta. You remember that as a child in 1940 you went there to visit family members who had been imprisoned in the nationalist movement. You visited the poet Rabindranath Tagore.

Tagore was very much a revered figure throughout India. He was an internationalist. He gave prophetic warnings against nationalism. Tagore was very old then. There were a lot of people visiting him. He lay on a cot wearing a white robe. He spoke very clearly, put his hands on my head, and said something like, "Be a good boy." That's about all I can remember. I discovered his work only recently, in the last six years or so. I'm astounded by how clear-headed he was.

You recall in the film that Hindu Muslim rioting broke out in your home state of Bihar in 1946 and that Mahatma Gandhi visited and took Hindu and Muslim children along with him through the devastated villages as an example of unity. You were one of those kids.

I traveled with Gandhi for about six weeks.

Did you have any personal contact, any kind of impression?

I had daily contact. I wish my mind had been clearer then, as clear as it is now. At that time, at age twelve, I was very much in the grip of Pakistani nationalism and viewed Gandhi as an unfriendly politician because he was a Congress leader. I went because my mother and father had Congress connections. I was under the influence of my brothers, who had turned to the Muslim League. So, I think I was not in as much of a learning mood as I should have been. But some things were very clear. One was the continuous, almost infectious love in which people around Gandhi held him. He was obeyed and listened to because they loved him, not because he was charismatic or exuded power. He was a gentle figure. I'll tell you one story. . . .

My brothers had said to me as I was going, "Since you are going with Gandhi, you might as well ask him to teach you to write English." They said Gandhi writes superb English. Later on I would realize they were absolutely right. He wrote superbly. You see that in *My Experiments with Truth*.[26] So, I said, "Mahatmaji, my brothers have told me that you write superb English." "Oh, that's very kind of those boys." I said, "They have told me to learn from you the principles of learning good English." He said, "My boy, there is only one principle. Read the Bible over and over again, the King James version." He said, "I prefer the King James version." I will always think of that. If you read Gandhi's writings and speeches, there is a biblical quality to his English prose: simple, short sentences, simple narrative, homilies.

Was Gandhi aware that your father had been murdered essentially for giving Congress support?

He knew the family history.

Then you make a very painful decision. . . .

No, I didn't.

It wasn't painful for you? Leaving your mother behind must have been tough.

I didn't make any decisions. Decisions were made for me. I was thirteen years old. In India, you don't make decisions when you're thirteen.

Your brothers said, "You're going to Pakistan."

They said, "Move." I moved.

What did your mother have to say about that?

She was against any of them going. At one point in her anger she said, "Go if you must, but you must know that you have all become Muslim Zionists." She was angry about it.

What was her name?

Khatoon.

And your father's?

Rahman.

Did you see your mother again after you left?

Never.

When did she die?

She died in 1972. I saw her just before she died, but she was too ill to talk to me.

On that trek in that caravan that you joined from Irki, you walk along the Grand Trunk Road and arrive in Delhi at a fort that you have vivid memories of.

You saw that in the film. It's difficult to talk about it.

Because of the emotion?

It's hard. It was hard doing the film also. I've never written about these things. The filming is an easier experience because there's a crew and there's the impersonality of technology and cameras looking at you. So, you're kind of performing in a way, I suppose.

You remember Nehru visiting the fort.

He visited twice. He just asked all the refugees how things were and what their needs were. He heard complaints that we were very cold at night. A few hours later some blankets arrived. He was thoughtful.

MARX'S LEGACY

Let's move on. 1998 is the 150th anniversary of the Communist Manifesto. *There are various symposia and conferences being held around this event. What are your thoughts on the relevance of Karl Marx and his legacy today?*

First, Marx focused our attention on the poor and the working class. Second, Marx and Frederick Engels rather brilliantly warned of and chalked out the exploitative oppressive patterns of capitalist development and the workings of the capitalist system. That capitalism has not been defeated or changed and continues to demonstrate a great deal of resiliency and dynamism are both true and were actually argued by Marx rather consistently; but it doesn't take away from the fact that capitalism is an exceptionally unjust system. We still have to figure out how to do away with it, or at least its worst features. That challenge remains, and that challenge was posed by Karl Marx.

Finally, the biggest achievement of Marx and Marxism may have been to offer us the methodology of analyzing social and historical realities. I do not think anyone has so far come up with a substitute for historical materialism as an explanation for the turns of history, the processes of history. Nor has anyone elaborated the idea of dialectics into a methodological system in the way that Marx and Marxism did. These are not mean achievements. These are high achievements, and were made within the context of focusing the minds of the educated class, or at least a certain sector of it, on peoples other than themselves—the poor, the working class, the oppressed, the weak, even the distant ones. This had never happened before.

The history of humanity is replete with the rejection of the Other. It is replete with callousness toward the Other, toward the habit of and traditions of and the intellectual outlook of that which is not you or not yours. Marx and Marxism focused the intelligentsia's attention in a positive way on the Other, the poor, the weak. And at least a section of the intellectual class, the intelligentsia as a whole, students, others, saw it as their moral and intellectual responsibility to comprehend reality in order to change it, to make the world better for all and not for themselves only. I don't think there had ever been such a class in history before. Once such a culture was created, you had a completely different view of producing literature and producing cinema, which we see, for example, in the films of Vittorio DeSica, Satyajit Ray, or, for that matter, people like Jean-Luc Godard. These are works of artists of the 1930s, 1940s, into the 1950s, replete with the idea of the Other viewed in positive, empathetic, and sympathetic ways. It introduced the notion of kindness, of a non-narcissistic outlook on life. These are not minor achievements. To the extent that these existed before Marx, to the extent they existed at all, they were associated with the religious person. This was the first time you saw secular intellect focus on issues of the common good.

How do you view the Asian meltdown? Starting in July 1997, Thailand, Malaysia, Indonesia, South Korea, and Japan all experienced serious economic decline.

First of all, I should admit that I haven't studied the Asian economic crisis very carefully. Having said that, I think we have to acknowledge that there is an internal crisis built into the capitalist system. This is too fast-moving a mechanism. It is too expansive a mechanism. It is too rapidly enlarging. In other words, it's in too fast a lane not to have breakdowns or major crashes. So, what happens in 1997 in East Asia, in Asia as a whole, is not really different from what happened in the 1930s in America. Since then, it has recurred as relatively manageable cycles of recession.

The difference here is that these were very vulnerable economies. They were often two-product economies. Korea produced electronics and automobiles. Malaysia was fundamentally an export-platform country. And so it went. In that situation, these economies were terribly sensitive to the economic currents elsewhere, in this case Japan. Once Japan ran into a recession, which is a common cold in capitalist economies, it hit the others with pneumonia. They catch cold and get pneumonia. They are more vulnerable. They don't have the capacity to withstand, for instance, pressures on their currency.

Mahathir Mohamad, the prime minister of Malaysia, reacted with great anger and panic to the collapse of Asian currencies by blaming George Soros, the Hungarian-born, U.S.-based financier. He immediately focused on him as the culprit. I don't know whether Soros had anything to do with this collapse or not, but what struck me as remarkable is that prime ministers, leaders of these countries that were being described as "tigers," would think that one currency speculator can pull their economy down that low. This was an indication of what they understood instinctively to be the extraordinary feebleness of their economic body.

It is also indicative of how wrongly and how badly world economists and institutions such as the World Bank and the International Monetary Fund exaggerated the successes of these East Asian economies. They should have known better. They should have seen that these were tigers standing on two legs. Stripes alone don't make tigers. But they didn't want to see that, which was really shocking, because it suggests that the compulsion to sell capitalism is so strong that they're willing to wrap all its ills in bright packaging and not tell the customer what might be wrong with it. That's bad business.

What accounts for capitalism's relative resilience, its ability to survive as an economic system?

It's a powerful system based on two important premises. One is that human beings are greedy. Greed is the strongest singular drive in the human animal. Greed for everything—money, power, accumulation, things to consume. The second is that reproduction is possible and good, and therefore, to organize for reproduction is the epitome of human endeavor. It's a very dynamic system. It takes unusual individuals who wouldn't be caught in it.

Have your perspectives on capitalism changed over the years as you've seen it ebb and flow?

My perspectives on capitalism have not changed. My perspectives on communism have changed. They have been changing over the last twenty-five or thirty years, slowly, gradually, but very surely. By 1972 or 1973, I was convinced, and I'm not bragging about it because it's in some of my writings, that the Soviet system was destined for failure, for two reasons. The Soviet leaders were ignoring some basic economic principles and were completely bypassing democratic governance. Democratic governance is central to the functioning of modern society; it can't function otherwise. These two failures on the part of the Soviet Union were very clear to me by the early 1970s.

I saw these not as Stalinist failures. I ran into some trouble over that one. I saw them as a failure that partly belongs to Marx and Engels. Marx always held the position that he was a scientist, not a prophet. Since the society of the future has never existed, he cannot outline its shape. He can as a scientist only examine that which can be observed. Fine, very good lines, hard to refute. But the truth is that if you're in the business of effecting change, then we have to take the risk of envisioning the future. It's not a scientific exercise, I'm sorry, but we have to engage in the artistic, political exercise of envisioning the future. The liberals did that much better.

For example, in Marx's extraordinary short statement in the *Eighteenth Brumaire*, he shied away from saying what shape communism would take.[27] There was some failure on the part of Marx and Engels, and his generation.

Then I think the big failure occurs with Lenin. Oh my God, in so many ways it would take hours to discuss it. First of all, the structure of Leninist thought, unlike that of Marx and Engels, is anti-democratic. We can hee or haw and try to get around it, but the manner in which Lenin envisioned the dictatorship of the proletariat, the notion of democratic centralism, and the idea of the avant-garde were all inherently anti-democratic. Democratic centralism sounded very democratic and therefore its articulation depended on what the Soviet Union, once the Bolshevik Revolution occurs, would do with the soviets. What they did was to control it from the top and destroy its autonomy. So, democratic centralism was more centralism than democratic. Actually what was practiced starting in 1919 and 1920, during the lifetime of Lenin himself, was centralist democracy, if you want to call it that, not democratic centralism. The centralist came first, democratic came second. Then you can go on and give a thousand excuses for it, the White revolution, the civil war, the attack on the Soviet revolution, the isolation that it suffered, the famines that followed, etc. But all that wouldn't explain the failure. It may justify it, but the failure remains. It was theoretical and intellectual. It lay in praxis. You can say praxis was not possible at that moment. That becomes an arguable point anyway.

It's like the American administration saying that you cut down on civil liberties when there is terrorism. It's always the argument of power. Then there were Lenin's personal tendencies to not tolerate dissent. Nikolai Bukharin was already in trouble. What Joseph Stalin did was to push trends that were discernible under Lenin beyond any reasonable limit. I say "beyond any reasonable limit." Lenin might have been shocked by them, but the trends were discernible in Lenin's time. After that, you have not had any serious Marxist thought until the Italian communist Antonio Gramsci. I think one of our difficulties lay in the fact that Gramsci was not taken seriously, and he was too obtuse to be understood all over the world. After Gramsci, I think most of our achievement of socialist movements, Marxist movements, lay in strategies and tactics related to wars of national liberation. We were really good at winning and consolidating them. We were very bad at taking them further. Somehow the Chinese have managed to survive, but at a fairly high price. I hope that during this anniversary of Marx that this will be an occasion for us to pull absolutely no punches and examine our failures brutally, honestly, and, more important, creatively. I think the achievements of the left have been very great. They have been, however, greater in the area of culture. The left transformed literature, art, and cinema more than actually changing societies.

For too long and too unjustly the Leninist left not merely criticized but condemned and rejected the social democrats of Europe as non-Marxist. That's not a just thing to do. I'm not trying to say that they are the best Marxists or the pure Marxists, but they are part of that labor and socialist tradition that came out of the social-democratic wing of the Marxist movement. They have achieved a great deal in terms of the betterment and the welfare of working people. That's not a small achievement.

What's your understanding of what's going on in Russia today?

Russia is struggling haphazardly to become a capitalist society. They plunged, with the collapse of socialism, into the culture of greed that capitalism entails without the other two components that make it a working system, that is, managerial organizational discipline and productive capabilities. The result is that Russia looks increasingly like a second-rate third-world country. It looks worse than Pakistan in many respects. We at least know how to manage some of the capitalist order; the Russians haven't got a clue. So, if there are three components to the dynamic of capitalism—greed, reproduction, and management—they have greed and not the others.

INTELLECTUAL WORK

One of your efforts is to establish Khaldunia, an alternative university in Pakistan. How is that coming along?

Not very well. I got off to a very good start in the first year, 1992 to 1993, because the press, the middle class, the government, and the industrialists all responded most positively. I was almost on the brink of getting the university started when the first government of Nawaz Sharif fell. Benazir Bhutto came into office in 1993 and seems to have come in with a grudge toward me. So it seems. I had written critically of her father's performance as prime minister. I very strongly opposed the regime of Zia ul-Haq and took risks for it, but in opposing the regime, I often pointed out that this tyranny was brought upon us by the blunders of Zulfikar Ali Bhutto. These are things that she must have disliked. But that isn't the real issue. The real issue is that she actually embraced a great number of the supporters of Zia ul-Haq, including some of his closest friends and allies.

Another problem was that now that Bhutto was in power, she felt deserved to be paid court. I was not paying court. Paying court is not something that suits my temperament. As a result, she dragged me out. The charter and the land didn't come through. She would make promises whenever editorials were written and people protested. Two or three times her government-controlled television would announce that everything had been done for Khaldunia and it was about to be opened; but actually nothing was being done. That's where it ended with three-and-a-half years of her rule. She broke my momentum. I lost a lot of credibility while I waited for her to act. She went out and Nawaz Sharif came back in.

When I returned to Pakistan after teaching a semester in the United States, I started all over again. I was making some progress, not as fast as before, when India tested its nuclear device last May. Pakistan followed suit two weeks later. During those two weeks, I traveled the country a great deal in an effort to prevent Pakistan testing. This didn't go very well with anyone. Since the tests, new sanctions have been imposed and the Pakistani economy has gone down very badly. I am sensing deep trouble. The country is going to have difficulty just getting through this period, much less being able to finance and support the founding of a new private university. I am going back and we'll see. We'll start all over again. I'm going to continue. I'm not giving up.

Do you have a sense, being outside the United States after living and working here for so many years, that your perspective on the country is changing?

Not really. I come. Often I spend two or three months each year in the United States. The country is changing. My perspective, I don't think, is changing very much. It's a country that has lost most of the gains that it had made from the New Deal, from the civil rights movement, and from the peace movement. These were major gains that I did not expect America to squander.

What do you attribute that to?

For one thing, those long years of Ronald Reagan and George Bush, but those long years themselves indicate that something had changed. Then the coming to office of someone as visionless and as unreliable as Bill Clinton. Finally, and it's important, this is too comfortable a country.

Where there is so much comfort possible, especially for radicals and former radicals, a softening with age essentially occurs. There are very few hard nuts that don't change, like Noam Chomsky or Howard Zinn. You can't expect everyone to be that tough.

Are you in that hard nut category?
That's for others to judge. Who am I to say?

In the BBC documentary about you, there's a wonderful poem, "Dawn of Freedom," by Faiz Ahmed Faiz, one of your favorite Urdu poets. What was your idea for putting that in?
I know of no third-world poet other than Faiz who was so prescient in catching the mood of disillusionment with the decolonized postcolonial states. He wrote this poem just about six months after India and Pakistan were independent. He in fact was talking of both of them. He saw with exceptional clarity the defective character of what we were at that time calling liberation, *azadi*, freedom. That makes it an extremely powerful poem.
The poem is translated by Agha Shahid Ali.

> These tarnished rays, this night-smudged light—
> This is not that Dawn for which,
> ravished with freedom,
> we had set out in sheer longing,
> so sure that somewhere in its desert
> the sky harbored a final haven for the stars,
> and we would find it.
> We had no doubt that night's vagrant wave
> would stray towards the shore,
> that the heart rocked with sorrow
> would at last reach its port.
> . . .
> But the heart, the eye,
> the yet deeper heart—
> Still ablaze for the Beloved,
> their turmoil shines.
> In the lantern by the road
> the flame is stalled for news:
> Did the morning breeze ever come?

Where has it gone?
Night weighs us down,
it still weighs us down.
Friends, come away from this false light.
Come, we must search for that promised Dawn.[28]

There's a famous couplet by Muhammad Iqbal. How about a translation of that?

That would be hard for me. Let me try. "For a thousand years, nargis," which is a rare flower, "weeps for its lack of brilliance. With much difficulty in the garden there is born someone capable of seeing inside."[29]

NOTES

1   Molly Moore, "Indian Riot Destroys Mosque," *Washington Post*, December 7, 1992, p. A1.

2   *The Idea of Empire*, Francis Hanley and Tim May dirs., written by Edward W. Said, BBC Arena, 1992; and *Stories My Country Told Me: With Eqbal Ahmad on the Grand Trunk Road*, H.O. Nazareth dir., BBC Arena/Penumbra, 1996.

3   See, for example, Benny Morris, *The Birth of the Palestinian Refugee Problem, 1947–1949* (Cambridge: Cambridge University Press, 1987); Ilan Pappé, *The Making of the Arab-Israeli Conflict, 1947–1951* (New York: St. Martin's Press, 1992); and Simha Flapan, *The Birth of Israel: Myths and Realities* (New York: Pantheon Books, 1987).

4   See, for example, Edward W. Said, "The One-State Solution," *New York Times Magazine*, January 10, 1999, p. 6: 36.

5   See, for example, Eqbal Ahmad's articles in the *New York Times* on March 28, 1979; April 15, 1979; April 25, 1979; and May 23, 1979.

6   Editorial, "Striking Against Terrorism," *New York Times*, August 21, 1998, p. A22.

7   See Eqbal Ahmad, "Terrorism: Theirs and Ours," Alternative Radio, October 12, 1998. Available from Alternative Radio (see Appendix).

8   Robert Fisk, "The Saudi Connection," *The Independent*, August 9, 1998, p. 19.

9   Prem Shankar Jha, "What's Behind the India-Pakistan Arms Race," *International Herald Tribune*, May 30, 1998, p. 6.

10 John F. Burns, "Pakistan, Answering India, Carries Out Nuclear Tests," *New York Times*, May 29, 1998, p. A1.

11 Akbar Ahmed, *Jinnah, Pakistan, and Islamic Identity: The Search for Saladin* (New York: Routledge, 1997).

12 "Unilateral Muscle-Flexing in a Unipolar World," *Dawn* 52: 227 (August 23, 1998): 15. See Eqbal Ahmad, "Missile Diplomacy," *The Nation* 267: 8 (September 21, 1998): 29.

13   See, for example, James Risen, "To Bomb Sudan Plant, or Not: A Year Later, Debates Rankle," *New York Times*, October 27, 1999, p. A1.

14   Eqbal Ahmad, "Comprehending Terror," *Middle East Report* 16: 3 (May–June 1986): 3–5.

15   John Kifner, "Hijacking of Flight 847: A Grisly Account," *New York Times*, June 17, 1985, p. A10.

16   Thomas L. Friedman, "Angry, Wired and Deadly," *New York Times*, August 22, 1998, p. A15.

17   David M. Anderson, quoted in Philip Shenon, "Hitting Home: America Takes on a Struggle with Domestic Costs," *New York Times*, August 23, 1998, p. 4: 1.

18   Tim Weiner, "Iran Said to Test Missile Able to Hit Israel and Saudis," *New York Times*, July 23, 1998, p. A1.

19   See Frantz Fanon, *The Wretched of the Earth*, trans. Constance Farrington (New York: Grove Press, 1968), pp. 148–205.

20   The Modern Library listed *A House for Mr. Biswas* (New York: Penguin, 1993) and *A Bend in the River* (New York: Vintage, 1989) as two of the 100 best novels of the century. See http:// www.randomhouse.com/modemlibrary/100best/ novels.html.

21   V.S. Naipaul, *Among the Believers: An Islamic Journey* (New York: Random House, 1982).

22   V.S. Naipaul, *Beyond Belief: Islamic Excursions Among the Converted Peoples* (New York: Vintage, 1998), p. xi.

23   Eqbal Ahmad, "Feudal Culture and Violence (Roots of Violence in Pakistan) II," *Dawn* 52: 31 (February 2, 1998): 13.

24   "The Great Day":

Hurrah for revolution and more cannon shot;
A beggar upon horseback lashes a beggar upon foot;
Hurrah for revolution and cannon come again,
The beggars have changed places but the lash goes on.

In William Butler Yeats, *The Poems: A New Edition*, ed. Richard J. Finneran (New York: Macmillan, 1983), p. 312. See also page xxxiv, note 8 (above).

25   See note 2.

26   Mahatma Gandhi, *An Autobiography: The Story of My Experiments with Truth*, trans. Mahadev H. Desai (New York: Dover Publications, 1983).

27   Karl Marx, *The Eighteenth Brumaire of Louis Bonaparte* (New York: International Publishers, 1964).

28   Faiz Ahmed Faiz, "Dawn of Freedom." See complete text in Urdu and translation (pp. viii–ix).

29   Muhammad Iqbal, *Kulliyat-e-Iqbal* (Aligarh: India, 1975), p. 268. Translation by Eqbal Ahmad and David Barsamian.

CHAPTER THREE

DO NOT ACCEPT
THE SAFE HAVEN

OPPRESSION AND IDENTITY

The argument is made that the Jewish people have been persecuted historically for millennia and have only one homeland: Israel. On the other hand, there are more than twenty Arab states. The Palestinians could go to any one of them, speak Arabic, and be culturally at home. How do you respond to that?

This is a polemical argument. It's very difficult to respond to it without sounding polemical. It is a historical fact that the Jewish people suffered unique forms of persecution all over Europe. They confronted prejudices even in the United States until very recently. It is also historically known and fully recognized by the best of Jewish scholars that, in relative terms, Jews had a much better time in the Islamic world. So that right up to the nineteenth century we spoke of the Judeo-Arab civilization in the same way as during the last half of the twentieth century we speak of the Judeo-Christian civilization. European anti-Semitism, which was not anti-Semitism of the Arabs, climaxed in the Holocaust. If the establishment of a Jewish nation within a specific territory and statehood was called for because of this persecution, it should have occurred in the Western world—in America or Europe—and not in the Arab world. The Arabs were not guilty of persecuting the Jews. The guilt was here, and therefore its expiation should have occurred here. I don't believe that expiation is a proper answer to such problems, but if expiation was needed, perhaps the Allies could have decided that a Jewish state would be founded in a part of Germany. Or they could have decided that it would be in a part of Poland or America. Why displace the Palestinians, who have lived in Palestine for more than 2,000 years, who have tilled that soil, who have built cities there, why displace them to accommodate the guilt of Europe? That's one answer. Sounds polemical.

But my real answer is that statehood, nationhood, is not a solution to the problems of our time. Black people have been persecuted here for a very long time. They were brought in as slaves. They were kept as indentured labor. They have remained in one way or another discriminated against in this country. Is the answer the creation of a black state in the South? Shall we turn Alabama and Mississippi into two black nations? No. The answer is: end the discrimination, overcome the prejudices, bring about integration of two peoples, restore democratic rights, create binational states, and build multicultural entities. The answer to evil is removal of evil, not its consolidation into statehoods.

So, you create a Jewish state. What comes out of it? What comes out of it, really, is a state in which I honestly think any self-respecting American or European Jew would not want to live. I will tell you why. If the United States had laws that Israel has, no self-respecting Jew would live here. It would discriminate against the Jews. They would not be able to buy property in the same way as the Christians do. They would not be able to join the army. They would not work in the civil service. In Israel today there are two categories of citizens. There are Jews and Arabs. The Arabs are third-class citizens without all the citizenship rights that Jews enjoy. Is that a statehood that the Jews would like to have here? The answer is no. I wouldn't want any Jewish person or black person or Muslim person to live in an America that discriminates against them. The solution is multi-culturalism, binationalism, and equality of citizenship. It's not exclusionary statehoods.

I understand what you're saying theoretically, but let me inject a personal note. My parents went through the Armenian genocide. As a result, because they were persecuted for being Armenian, their identity became hyper-extended. They became much more conscious of their language, religion, and culture. It seems that when a people is targeted for genocide, the sense of tribalism increases. You have no friends, no allies. You need to be able to stick with your own. That's what I felt with a lot of the Armenians that I knew growing up.

That's totally right. But I really think it would have been a great tragedy for the Armenians if they had responded by establishing, say, an Armenian nation in a part of Turkey. What would have happened is that such a state would be at war with Turkey even today. What you have today is an Armenian people conscious of that proud and sad history. This tragedy has steeled them to understand and hold on to traditions in a world of multiple cultures. There are French Armenians and American Armenians and Lebanese Armenians. They all share a number of common things that unite them as one people universally, one people in many nations. They have a common culture, including the memory of a common tragedy. In this sense, I do not support even the establishment of a Palestinian state.

If it's exclusionary.

In fact, I'm still wishing that the Palestinians will find a way to live with Jews. Jews in particular, because they are now part of Palestine. That is why I believe that the only future for Palestine is Jewish and Palestinian multinationality.

Edward Said has commented that it's ironic that the Palestinians have become the victim of the victims.[1]

It is ironic, but history is full of ironies. This is one of the biggest ones.

Cut through some of the lexical cobwebs that surround the Middle East. Arabs who are critical of Israel are called anti-Semitic.

This is pure propaganda. Arabs are Semites and speak a Semitic language. If you look at the image of the Arab in America, as well as in many Western European countries, the Arab is actually the shadow of the Jew.

In what way?

The caricatures of the Jew that used to appear in Western cartoons, all the adjectives that used to appear in Western literature before the Holocaust, are now being applied to the Arabs. A typical cartoon in America shows the Arab with a long, hooked nose. It's an unmistakably Semitic nose. During the oil crisis of 1973 to 1975, the Arab was continually portrayed as very rich and very greedy. That portrayal still exists. Not very long ago that was the image of the Jew. In the lexicon of popular language of America and the West, today's Arab is yesterday's Jew.

Secretary of State Madeleine Albright says that terrorism is "the war of the future."[2] *One of your lectures is entitled "Terrorism: Theirs and Ours."*[3] *The former should be familiar to most people. What might "our terrorism" be?*

I argue among other things that "our" terrorism and "theirs" converge. They converge so deeply and so frequently that often it becomes difficult to know who is who. In 1986, I was writing with Richard Barnet a long piece on the Afghanistan war for *The New Yorker*.[4] The very month that we were drafting our essay a delegation of Afghan *mujahideen* arrived at the White House. They were warmly received and praised by President Ronald Reagan.[5] In 1988, this holy war of the Muslims, financed by the U.S. government to the tune of $8 billion, was over. As soon as it ended, the United States took its profit and came home. The "evil empire" was weakened and tottering. The *mujahideen* were then transformed into terrorists. In 1998, their camps were hit by American missiles.[6] So you see the convergences.

In the current issue of The Progressive, *you say, "Osama bin Laden is a sign of things to come."*[7] *What do you mean by that?*

The United States has sowed in the Middle East and in South Asia very poisonous seeds. These seeds are growing now. Some have ripened, and others are ripening. An examination of why they were sown, what has grown, and how they should be reaped is needed. Missiles won't solve the problem.

POETRY AND REVOLUTION

Let's change direction. Talk about the Sufi tradition in the subcontinent.

The mystical tradition in Islam is known as Sufism.[8] Those who follow that tradition are known as Sufis. The word comes from *suf*, which means "wool." These people originally wore very simple, coarse, woven woolen clothing—hence "Sufi," those who wear coarse clothing. I should say that there is a misconception arising out of Orientalist literature on Islam in India that the people of India converted in large numbers to Islam as a result of coercion: "Islam is spread by the sword." This is an incorrect impression. The spread of Islam in the subcontinent is the work of the Sufis, who preached by their example. By and large, they were not proselytizers. They were people who went and lived in the community, Hindu and Muslim, and served it. They lived by service and by setting an example of treating people equally without discrimination. Since India was divided so rigidly by caste, they appealed particularly to the untouchables, the lowest Hindu caste. The Sufis offered social mobility, as well as dignity and equality to the poor.

You find in the subcontinent a great deal of Sufi worship. Nearly every part of India, Pakistan, and Bangladesh has a shrine. My village had one. Typically members of both communities, Hindus and Muslims, will celebrate the birth or the death anniversary of that particular saint whose shrine it is.

What are your views on religion?

I am very harshly secular. But let's be clear about what "secular" means to me, and ought to mean generally to everybody else. In its original meaning, it doesn't mean that you are irreligious or that you are opposed to religion. Secular to me means that the laws of the state, the laws of society, will not be enacted in accordance with some divine injunction; they will be enacted in response to the needs of society. Law treats everyone equally—be they Christians, Jews, Hindus, or Muslims—and is made for everyone equally. That's secular to me. It's in that sense that to me Israel is not a secular state, nor is Pakistan, but the United States is.

What's the distinction between mazhab *and* ruhaniyat?

"*Mazhab*" refers to following a certain form, to ritual, to rules. "*Ruhaniyat*" refers to the spirit of religion, its essence, its internalization rather than form. So, when a Muslim is praying five times, he is following a *mazhab*. When a Hindu goes to the temple every morning and makes offerings, he or she is following a *mazhab*. When you are seeing signs of the divine or living out spiritually, morally, the life of a Muslim or a Hindu as you understand the spirit of your religion, that's *ruhaniyat*.

I think I am Muslim in the sense that I am not at all concerned with form. I am much more concerned with spirit. Spirit means certain things to me. The universal in Islamic civilization is important to me. The emphasis on developing the internal resources of persons is important. The emphasis on a higher morality is very important. The sources of these values for me are both secular and religious. They are simultaneously Islamic and philosophically learned from studying secular Islamic and secular Western literature.

There are several Iqbal couplets that I'd like to discuss with you. Let's take one of his famous ones: "Love plunged into Nimrod's fire without hesitation. Meanwhile, reason is on the rooftop, just contemplating the scene."[9] *Here Iqbal is saying something very powerful about love versus intellect.*

This is Sufi thought, Islamic mystical thought. It's also true, by the way, of Christian, Jewish, and Hindu mysticism. All mysticisms have some common features. In Islamic mystical thought, there are pairings. There is a continuous dialectical interplay of opposites—not just one, but a whole set of them. *Zahir* and *batin*. That which is apparent and that which is hidden. Visible versus invisible. Good versus evil. *Ishq*, love, versus *aql*, reason. The conception is that there is a continuous interplay of these opposing realities, the reality of love and the reality of reason, within the human being. The reality of the visible, perceived, versus the unperceived, the felt. Human personality attains its greatness as it learns, as it trains itself, to resolve these contradictions within itself.

In Sufi thought, love, always takes precedence over reason. Iqbal is saying here that love jumped into the fire of Nimrod to oppose him without a sense of danger, without fear, while reason is still watching from the sidelines. The couplet means that there are certain situations in which love must overcome reason and logic. The pattern and contrast are classic.

One of the things that struck me when I lived in India was how people who would be technically described as illiterate would recite poems by Iqbal or Mir Taqi Mir or Mirza Ghalib or Faiz with considerable skill.

Let me react to that remark of yours with a personal story. When I was four years old, I witnessed a very severe violence, the killing of my father. After that, I was not prepared mentally for the rigors of learning. The doctors advised that I shouldn't be sent to school. So, at that time my brother argued there was no need for me to be schooled. In fact, his sentence was that we are still living in a society which is illiterate but educated. What he meant by that is exactly what you are saying. We were living in rural areas, and the large majority of India's poor people, Hindus and Muslims, could not read and write. But most Hindus could recite the *Mahabharata*, and the great epics, by heart. Most Muslims could not only recite the *Quran*, but more importantly, could recite and remember a large number of fables and epics, the *Arabian Nights*, and such poets as you mentioned. Poetry is deeply seeped into the lives of people. Poetry in the subcontinent and also in the Middle East, and all over the Islamic world, is very much integrated as part of life.

*In terms of political verse, Iqbal's "Farishton ka Geet" ("Song of the Angels"),
is a real call to arms.*

> *Rise up, wake up the poor of the world.*
> *Shake up the palaces of the rich and the powerful.*[10]

That's the revolutionary in him. Iqbal is very much a product of a
transition. He stands right on the brink of the shift from tradition to
modernity. He is a traditional Sufi poet, as well as a modern nationalist
poet and a modern revolutionary poet. The traditional influence on him
is quite consistent and without contradictions. He is a Sufi. The modern influence on him is full of the contradictions of modernity. He is a
Marxist; he is a Muslim nationalist; and he is also an Indian nationalist.
Therefore, he produces continuously fairly contradictory strains. He is
as contradictory as the modern man of the first decades of the twentieth century. "Song of the Angels" is greatly influenced by revolutionary
waves of Europe, which had then started to blossom in Asia.

PATHOLOGIES OF POWER

One of the terms you've coined is "pathologies of power" in postcolonial states.[11]
What do you mean by that?

By that I mean the fact that third-world politicians and institutions,
individuals who hold power and the institutions they run, do not express
themselves most of the time in reasonable ways.

Saddam Hussein of Iraq requiring typewriters to be licensed is pathological. Saudi Arabia opening universities, which is a good thing, but
fearing that the students shouldn't get together—because they might
talk politics or revolt—and therefore doing everything to prevent the
students from discussing matters, from meeting together, and from collaborating—this is the exact reverse of what universities should be.

Third-world writers are among the most endangered species in the
world. Nearly all Arab writers today are living in exile of one form
or another. The only great novelist Saudi Arabia has ever produced in
its entire history is Abdelrahman Munif. He has been divested of his
citizenship. It is as if a body politic, a social body, is cutting itself off
from something important, something creative. Munif lives in exile in
Damascus. Adonis, another important writer, is a Syrian. He lives in
exile in Paris or sometimes in Beirut. In Pakistan, since independence, I
think there has not been a major literary figure who has not served time

in prison. To me these are all examples of sickening behavior on the part of the state which expresses an illness, a pathology. These are not natural ways of behaving.

There's the case also of the Bangladeshi writer Taslima Nasrin.

Taslima Nasrin is one of the recent examples of what is happening. This is not normal, especially when you think of the fact that most of these writers, a majority of them, are really not saying or doing anything that is threatening. Taslima Nasrin is not a great writer. She wrote a novel in which she portrays the risks that the Hindu minority runs in a majority Muslim Bangladesh.[12] She is alleged to have given an interview in which she said something to the effect that she does not believe that the traditions of the prophet Muhammad are binding on Muslims. Whether she said it or not, we do not know. She denies it, and for that she's been driven out.[13] These are all pathological behaviors.

I can cite many more. Benazir Bhutto, in the space of three and a half years as prime minister, stole nearly $2 billion from a poor country like Pakistan. That's pathology. She doesn't need that kind of money. She was already a rich woman.

Nawaz Sharif says that he thinks the introduction of sharia, *Islamic law, would be a good thing for Pakistan.*[14]

I wrote about this as soon as Sharif proposed a fifteenth amendment to the constitution. I argued that Islam has been, in Pakistan and also in other Muslim countries, a refuge for weak and scoundrel regimes and rulers in modern times. Whenever they feel threatened and isolated— and are losing their grip, losing popularity, and losing the consensus of the people—they bring out Islam from the closet and use it as a political weapon. That's what Nawaz Sharif is doing. He has been in office now for nearly two years. Pakistan's economy has not improved. It's in very bad shape. He tested nuclear weapons and Pakistan's security has not improved. The perception of security has not improved. Our basic disputes with India have not been resolved. He supported the Taliban in Afghanistan, which has brought us in conflict with Iran, as if we needed one more hostile neighbor. And there are very serious allegations now, starting with an article that appeared in the London *Observer*, that in his first government in 1990 he had stolen a lot of money and transferred it to foreign banks.[15] Under these conditions, Sharif pulls Islam out from the closet and he starts the process of "Islamization." This is a typical use of religion for political purposes.

At the United Nations, both the Pakistani and Indian prime ministers announced their intention to sign the Comprehensive Test Ban Treaty.[16] *What did you make of that?*

I think they will sign it. Washington, after decades of refusing to stop testing its own advanced nuclear weapons, has finally decided that there could be a Comprehensive Test Ban Treaty (CTBT). Therefore, Washington has now become deeply committed to getting all the nuclear countries to sign it. Getting Pakistan and India to sign it is considered to be very important. But it's a meaningless gesture. The CTBT commits a country to not test its weapons, but testing is not essential nowadays. With advanced computer systems, cold tests are yielding as much information as a real-life test used to do. So, that's one problem. The other is that the terms of the treaty are such that any country written into the treaty can get out of it the moment it wants to do so. There's nothing binding about it. India and Pakistan would sign the treaty, provided the United States lifts the economic and technological embargo that it has put on India and Pakistan. It would be to both countries' advantage. But that does not end the arms race between India and Pakistan.

SRI LANKA

What is your analysis of the ongoing conflict in Sri Lanka?

The start of this conflict had the same logic as the partition of India in 1947. Sinhalese nationalism developed in the 1920s, 1930s, and 1940s. It tended to invest Sri Lankan nationalism with exclusively Buddhist Sinhalese memory, Sinhalese symbols, Sinhalese rituals, and Sinhalese texture, thus giving the Tamils, who are a minority, the feeling of being excluded from the mainstream Sri Lankan nationalism. A demand is being made of the Tamils to drop their identity in favor of a Sinhalese identity if they want to remain proper Sri Lankan citizens. That's how it's perceived.

Roughly something similar happened much earlier in India. The emergence of Hindu nationalism started investing into Indian nationalism the symbols, the values, and the rituals of Hinduism rather than the syncretic Indo-Muslim civilization that had developed over a 700-year period. It became exclusionary in its content, an exclusively Hindu rather than that multicultural nationalism, if one can call it that. The result was that Muslims reacted to this with their own nationalist feelings. A similar thing has happened with the Tamils. The emergence of Tamil nationalism was in large part a reaction to the Sinhalization of Sri Lankan nationalism in the 1920s, 1930s, and 1940s.

Then in 1983, something quite horrible happened. In major cities, particularly in Colombo, the capital of Sri Lanka, large-scale rioting occurred in which Tamils were killed in large numbers just for being Tamils. That rioting alienated the Tamil population from the Sinhalese majority in a very significant way. It is in that setting, after the 1983 riots, that you see the beginnings of the rise of the Liberation Tigers of Tamil Eelam (LTTE). The LTTE is a violent and armed terrorist organization that demanded a separation of the Tamil majority area in the northern part of the island from the rest of Sri Lanka. So the two-nation theory begins to develop. Now in Sri Lanka there are two nations, one Tamil, the other Sinhalese.

The LTTE has now acquired a life of its own. In my view, it probably does not have the support of an overwhelming majority of Tamils living in Sri Lanka. But it has become institutionalized as a violent nationalist organization that continues to demand separate statehood. The local Tamils are less supportive of LTTE than the expatriate community.

By the way, lots of interesting things are happening in the world. Migration is changing the nature of nationalism all over the world. There are large Sri Lankan communities in Canada, the United States, and Britain. Many of them are Tamils who sympathize with the LTTE. Therefore, a lot of money is flowing to the Tigers from the expatriate community. Presently, the Tigers are holding the coastal areas and are engaged on a very large scale in the trade of drugs and arms, which are international trading items these days. So, a lot of income is coming from that. They have proven, therefore, to be a fairly resilient armed organization, one that is hard to defeat. For the last two and a half years, the Sri Lankan government has held Jaffna, the main city in the Tamil-majority area. They have been able to elect mayors in fairly free elections, but the LTTE has been in a position to knock them off, to assassinate them. So the violence and counter-violence, terror and counter-terror, has become so woven into the fabric of Sri Lankan life today that it is difficult to foresee a way out of it.

Do you see partition as a viable option?

I don't see partition as a viable option, but so far there seems to be no sign of the LTTE and the Sri Lankan government negotiating an end to this horror. The government of President Chandrika Kumaratunga has pursued a policy, in the last three years that she has been in power, of being tough and also open to negotiations. She has been offering what appear to be relatively good terms to the Tamils for resettlement, autonomy, and greater control of the Tamil-held regions. Those proposals are on the table. But the LTTE is not biting. At the same time, Kumaratunga has also taken strong military initiatives as a way to bring the Tamils to the table. Her policy of being soft on negotiations and hard on the military front so far has not worked.

ETHNIC CONFLICT IN THE BALKANS

Let's move to another area of conflict. The conventional wisdom is that during the period of Soviet rule, within the Soviet Union itself and its allied states, nationalist impulses and separatist tendencies were contained by Soviet power. With the collapse of the USSR, those nationalisms came to the fore, in the Caucasus and in the Balkans, particularly. Do you distance yourself from that conventional analysis?

To a certain extent, yes, but not entirely. There is little doubt that the collapse of communism in the Soviet Union and Eastern Europe created an environment in which ethnic nationalism could thrive. But this in itself is not really at the heart of the matter. Some conflicts, like the one in Chechnya, are clearly identifiable that way. The Chechens felt discriminated against within Russia. They rose in revolt, first demanding autonomy and eventually independence. They have negotiated some sort of an end to the conflict, partly because the Russian state is so weak it couldn't continue with its military operations, and partly because there was some sensibility on both sides to reach some sort of agreement.

In the case of the Balkans, the matter is a bit more complex, isn't it? Slobodan Milosevic, the Serbian leader of Yugoslavia, is a die-hard old-style fascist. He is also an ambitious politician, very much in the manner of Hitler. He saw Yugoslavia as being in crisis after the collapse of communism, sensed a vacuum, and used it to arouse the worst aspects of Serbian nationalism. The worst aspect means that he wanted to mobilize Serbs' hatred of Croats and Muslims. Milosevic began by mobilizing

Serbs' hatred of Muslims from Kosovo in the late 1980s. He built his power base from Kosovo.

The reason why such horrors occurred in the Balkans is that the intended victims of Milosevic happened to be Muslims, largely. The West is less concerned about Muslims than it is about Christians, for example. There is a sectarian quality to the emotional makeup of the West that I have found difficult to grasp—its continuity, its strong roots. . . . Like racism, anti-Muslim feelings linger in Western thought and political culture. That contributed to it.

A second factor in this crisis was the reunification of Germany in 1990 and the collapse of an adversarial relationship with Russia. The former brought out, in the Western European psyche particularly, the old fears of the rise of Germany. Those fears were particularly strong in Britain and France. Therefore, when Germany accorded recognition to Croatia in December 1991, those fears were further augmented. "My God, the Germans are expanding their sphere of influence, and we have to find the old balancing mechanisms that had defined European politics since the Treaty of Westphalia." That is, you have to balance Germany with Russia. Therefore, a tendency developed to allow Russia to expand its influence in what is called lesser Slavia, that is, the Serb areas. The Russian sympathy for the Serb cause prevented the West from seeing that Serbia was, in fact, engaged in genocide. Well, they saw it, but they did not want to do anything about it.

To this day, I see editorials asking why are we still trying to deal with Milosevic when we all know that he's untrustworthy. Milosevic is a fascist. He has never kept a promise. He has always manipulated. Why is Washington still negotiating with him? The reason is that the United States wants a strong Serbia intact so that it could be a balancing mechanism, along with Russia, against a possible strong Germany.

That's the geopolitical consideration.

Unfortunately, I think it's a fictional one. We probably haven't quite explained it. The politics of the nineteenth and the early twentieth centuries is not the politics of the twentieth and the twenty-first centuries. The central problem of our times is that the political minds of decision-makers remain rooted in the past. And the logic of the past has changed. Modern technology, the modern economy, and modern ideologies have changed it. But we still view Europe in terms of balance-of-power politics.

If Germany is united, we must find balancing mechanisms against it. We must have America continue to take an interest in Europe. Therefore, we have the expansion of the North Atlantic Treaty Organization in the 1990s. Its expansion frankly made no other sense except in those terms.

Let's suppose that in Banja Luka, a town in Bosnia, sixteen synagogues or sixteen churches were destroyed. What might have been the reaction to that? I should add that sixteen mosques were in fact destroyed in Banja Luka.[17]

The numbers themselves do not say very much. The mosque of Ferhat Pasha, by far the best-known example of Islamic architecture in Europe, was completely razed in 1993.[18] The analogy would be to ask: how would we react if some nationalist cause in Europe had destroyed the church of Francis of Assisi or the great cathedral in Rome? There would have been an outrage. Think of the National Library in Sarajevo, which has been totally destroyed by Serb bombings. It held one of the best collections of medieval Islamic and Jewish manuscripts. Nobody cared very much. It's a great national library of Europe, razed to the ground. All of its books have been burned. This has happened in the last decade of the twentieth century, and the world has behaved as if nothing abnormal occurred. Or, for that matter, take the case of what happened in Srebrenica, right in the presence of the U.N. peacekeeping forces. Thousands of people were massacred in three or four days.[19] These things have been quite extraordinary. They happened at a time when I thought they couldn't possibly happen.

Almost parallel to the war in the Balkans, particularly Bosnia, events were going on in Rwanda of even more horror and atrocity.[20]

The same kind of indifference, callous disregard prevailed for a very, very long time. When they attend to it, they attend too late. Look at Kosovo. As I said earlier, it is from here that Milosevic launched his politics of hatred in the late 1980s and begins the campaign of ethnic cleansing, a mobilization of hate he calls Serbian nationalism. Since 1991, as we were witnessing genocide in Bosnia, every knowledgeable commentator on the region has said that we need to look at the problem of Kosovo. One day or another, another round of ethnic cleansing by the Milosevic regime is going to break out. Now is the time to attend to resolving the problem. Milosevic proceeds to annul the autonomy of the Kosovo province and proceeds to impose military and police rule on Kosovo—with the whole world watching—until the genocide begins.

INTERNATIONAL SOLIDARITY

When you look at the current world scene, might you suggest some resistance strategies to the neoliberal agenda?

Resistance strategies presuppose a constituency of resistance. I'm having difficulty identifying the constituencies of resistance. Take the case of Bosnia. All genocides of modern times have had a defining symbol. The defining symbols of Hitler's genocide of Jews and gypsies were the concentration camp and the gas chambers. The defining symbols of the genocide in Bosnia were the concentration camps and the rape camps. This is the first time that rape was used as an organized weapon of ethnic warfare. This happened in the early 1990s, when in the Western world particularly, the women's movement was at its height. Take an example. Bill Clinton ran his first presidential campaign on a promise of lifting the embargo on the Bosnians. The arms embargo was hurting the Bosnians and not the Croats and not the Serbs, who were attacking them. He also had advocated a policy of lift and strike, that is, lifting the embargo and carrying on air strikes on Serb artillery that was shelling Sarajevo. Of course, Clinton didn't fulfill his promise; but a month after he had come into the White House, the various parts of the United States women's movement organized a large march on Washington for reproductive rights. I had kind of expected that there the issue of rape camps would become central. President Clinton and his wife received a representative delegation of women from the march. That delegation did not even mention rape camps or Bosnia. So, here was a mobilized group of people conscious about the necessity of protecting rights, and it neglected a very important issue concerning women. By sheer contrast, I must mention an exception.

A few weeks later, the Holocaust Museum was opened in Washington, D.C. Clinton came to inaugurate it. To their credit, Jewish leaders, one after another, in their speeches, including the welcoming speech to President Clinton, emphasized the necessity of doing something to stop this genocide. I shall always be grateful to these people for speaking up.

So, to come back to your question, I am first wondering how should we rehabilitate a consciousness of international solidarity among people who should have it naturally. I think that has to be somehow restored. Women marching in Washington in hundreds of thousands for their rights and not mentioning Bosnia at a time when that genocide was at a climax suggests that consciousness of international solidarity has receded from these people's movements. It has to be restored. That's the first step. Why has it receded? What are the roots of its recession? It may be the end of the fear of war between Russia and America, or the end of the fear over nuclear weapons. Those are factors that may have added to it. Previously every international conflict or crisis had the message built into it of possibly being a trip wire for a nuclear holocaust. That trip wire has been removed. But the solidarity shouldn't be removed as a result.

MARKETING INDIVIDUALISM

Freud talked about something he called "the narcissism of minor differences."[21]
Do you think that may be at play here?

It is definitely at play. The problem I think is much larger than that, namely, the movement that we belong to, of which we are children in many ways, the 1960s, was narcissistic. The culture of narcissism itself is very prevalent in American society today. It may also be true of Europe, but I don't know Europe so well. Its roots are in capital, in consumerism. Switch on your television. All the advertisements are about your individual comfort, consumption, and pleasure. It is drilled into children and adults day in and day out. It has an effect that shapes our minds. The notion of solidarity beyond self and beyond family, beyond the small group, has become increasingly alien in modern consumer-oriented American society.

Let's take this a little further. The relationship of people to the economic environment has changed in many ways. In the agrarian, pre-modern, pre-industrial society, man was a unit of cooperation. The agrarian mode of production demanded that people cooperate to survive and to produce. When harvest time came, the entire village helped each other in harvesting faster than a single family could do it. The same was true of seeding time. Or when floods arrived, you needed a communal response. That particular mode of production emphasized the role of men and women as units of cooperation. Cooperation was essential to that particular political culture and environment.

Then you move toward industrialism. In the industrial age, the individual became important as a unit of production. Manufacturing was the central objective of the political economy. Here you are treating the individual as a unit of production. You are interested in the individual's skills. You are interested in the individual's productivity. Therefore, you would notice that throughout the late nineteenth century and all of the first half of the twentieth century, if you look at the research outlay of big corporations, it was mostly spent on how to promote the individual's productivity. Timing, labor hours, development of skills, rhythm methods, lighting arrangements, all the research was on industrial production and how to increase productivity. Starting with the 1950s onward, there has been a shift. Corporations now spend much less on human beings as units of production and much more on human beings as units of consumption. The major research in most of the corporations is on how to sell, not how to produce.

The United States has a $7 trillion dollar economy. One trillion dollars, one-seventh of the economy, is spent on marketing.

When you are emphasizing the individual's role as a unit of production, you are interested in his external relationships, his skills, for example. You are interested in his ability to collaborate with others. Without collaboration, there can't be production. When you are emphasizing the individual's role as a consumer, you are interested really in focusing on that individual's self-centeredness, his or her sexuality and self-image, a parent's relationship to his or her children, the children's relationship to their parents, a wife's relationship to her husband, each person's relationship to their car, and so on. This whole exercise promotes concentration on self. It's trying to enter into your psyche and thus invade the privacy of the individual, which is a very totalitarian process. That is why I have always argued that the whole democratic process in the world today is threatened by the fact that major institutions of society are trying to enter into the private life of people to turn them into consumers. If I am interested in you as a consumer, I am interested in your relationship to your wife, your sexuality, your self-image. These are all internal. When external bodies of power enter into the private lives of individuals, that's where democracy stops and totalitarianism begins.

The other aspect of this process is that it promotes narcissism. It promotes a concentration and emphasis on self. Me, me, me. Us, us, us. We, we, we. That makes it difficult to have a genuine sense of solidarity. I spoke in 1994 to a group of American women about Bosnia. I was harsh because I considered them comrades. What struck me was that a couple of women were angry, but a majority left the meeting thoughtfully. So, our fundamental urges are still there to reach out to others, to hear and to show solidarity. But in this environment, it's getting harder and harder. We just have to make an effort.

Vandana Shiva has proposed the idea of "the recovery of the commons."[22] *She sees enclosures, the fencing off of common property, as a problem. What do you think of that?*

It's a good idea. What is needed is really a transformation in our way of looking at the environment. There is a lot about how badly the media treat a given subject, but what we really have to look into is the ways in which advertisements, corporations, the media insidiously are transforming the nature of our relationship to the environment in which we live. That's a major intellectual task in which very few of us have been engaged.

Do you think such environmental problems as ozone depletion and global warming might be a wedge to create a more universal solidarity? If global warming is happening in Pakistan, it's also happening in the United States and in Argentina.

You're absolutely right, but unless a sense of solidarity is widely shared, environmental concerns cannot and will not take on a global quality. Americans are the largest single consumers of raw materials in the world. The environmental movement in its activist phase is about ten years old. It has not made any dent on the patterns of American consumption. So, we speak of environment, but we are not willing to look at how our economies and our lives are affecting the environment. We care about the immediate needs of the environment, but we don't think about the Himalayas. We can't until consciousness changes. Instrumental approaches are important, but they are not sufficient.

What happens, then, to the individual who makes that shift from moving away from being absorbed in a self-indulgent consumerism, me-too-ism, to seeing the picture?

What happens? At the individual level your life is enriched. The question is: what do you do to translate it to a wider community, to convey this experience, to convey your values to others who matter, who we care about? You are doing it through the radio. You are doing it by transmitting information and ideas the best you can, and taking risks in the process. I really think that the notion of taking risks has to enter into our lives. If we do not take risks, we cannot serve the common good. The risk is often not taken, but the willingness to court it has to be there.

ANTONIO GRAMSCI AND ALBERT CAMUS

There are a couple of people that I want you to talk about. The first is Antonio Gramsci. In another interview, you said that he was not taken seriously and he was also too obtuse.[23] What is your appreciation of Gramsci?

I still learn from him. Gramsci remains one of the most important among the theoreticians of the twentieth century, more important than Michel Foucault and others who came after him. He has a grasp of class struggle, of the effect that power has on weakness, that wealth has on poverty, and the state has on civil society. He is also the only one of the major theoreticians of our time who actually came from a poor background. He is also the only one who was deeply engaged in a day-to-day struggle of people, the only one who spent long years and disintegrated in the suffering of prison. Those details have given a texture to his insights that are in so many ways unique. He remains very hard to read because his writing feels so disjointed and sometimes so obtuse. His writing is so episodic and so insightful that there are flashes of light coming in darkness and then there's darkness again. I often have to read the same article two or three times to get it.

To perhaps intersect with your comment about risks, there's the often cited Gramsci quote that one needs to have "Pessimism of the intellect and optimism of the will."[24]

This paradox is so good because what he is saying is that we live in a very shitty world. Critical intellect requires that we recognize the dirt around us, that we see it clearly but not be overwhelmed by it, and that we know that it can be cleaned up. If we don't, it will likely be much harder anyway. Pessimism of the intellect is a call to critical intellect. Pessimism of the intellect is a call to genuine realism in comprehending reality, and optimism is a call to the commitment to the common good. This is a paradox that's a creative paradox, from which good can come.

Another interesting figure is Albert Camus. He was born in Oran, Algeria. He was part of the anti-Nazi resistance and the democratic left in France. But he was very conflicted about his homeland, Algeria. He once said that in a world of victims and executioners, it's the job of thinking people not to be on the side of executioners.[25] *But when it came to the French in Algeria, he had a real problem.*

He remained very torn about it. His French nationalism and his social conscience were at war. When I look back, I think there was also an element of a rather culturally rooted conviction in him that it was good for Algeria to remain French. In nourishing that conviction, he was not realistic, because of a refusal to understand his own people and also Algerian aspirations. There was also a refusal to grasp the deep wounds that racial encounters inflict on people on both sides. It distorts both the victim and the victimizer. Algeria is still struggling with that distorted identity. So in a very strange way is France. It is not perhaps coincidental that France is being challenged by Jean-Marie Le Pen's fascist movement. Le Pen's National Front is gaining strength unexpectedly in French society. Algeria is suffering from Islamism, on the one hand, and militarism, on the other.

You spent three years in Algeria in the early 1960s.

In North Africa, not all of it in Algeria. Some of it in Algeria, some of it in Tunisia, and a very small part in Morocco. . . . I think those years were politically very formative for me. They were most probably intellectually less formative than Princeton was. Princeton was intellectually more formative because it threw at me ideas and concepts that I had to confront and react to. I think intellectually my oppositional outlook, to the extent that I have one, developed in Princeton. This was a time of conformity in America, and that conformity was very frightening. Orientalism was coming to a climax, which was very threatening in some ways. This period saw the emergence and consolidation of area studies in the American academy, which they are now struggling to save by hooking on to themes of globalization. I don't know if they will be able to save it or not.

DO NOT ACCEPT THE SAFE HAVEN

Tipoo Sultan was the last great opponent of British colonization of India. He was finally defeated by the British in 1799, actually by Arthur Wellesley who would later become the Duke of Wellington and defeat Napoleon. After that, there was no major resistance until the great uprising of 1857. At the time of his death, he gave some advice to his sons. Iqbal has put Tipoo Sultan's advice to his sons in poetry:

You are a wanderer by choice.
Do not accept the safe haven.
Even if Laila should be in it,
do not ride in that carriage.[26]

The reference is to the famous Islamic love story, *Laila and Majnun*. Majnun is filled with his desire for Laila, to the point that he goes crazy. She is the essence of beauty, fulfillment, and the comforts in life. Therefore, Laila has come to symbolize that finality of material attainment. However, the couplet warns that even if Laila is sitting in the *mahmel*, the camel carriage, don't ride.

It seems in some ways you too have in your practice spurned that promise of material wealth and the attraction of fame and acceptance.

You are being very kind. I think I have been very selfish in seeking my happiness. I am a very happy man in many ways.

I'm talking in the sense of ruhaniyat, spiritually rich.

I know what you are saying. What I said was that there was no sacrifice on my part. It has all been to my benefit. I don't own very much, but I'm rather happy.

A lot of people in the third world and in the United States are very appreciative of your efforts for so many years.

People are very kind and loving.

That was really manifest at an extraordinary weekend that was held at Hampshire College in early October 1997. A lot of your students, colleagues, confrères, and friends from all over the world and the United States, people like Noam Chomsky, Howard Zinn, Edward Said, and others, all gathered to literally celebrate your sense of solidarity and commitment. It was quite a moving event.

It was delightful, wasn't it? And funny at times, and very moving. But I think all of us, you too, run into that all the time. Last night I spoke at the University of Colorado here in Boulder. I noticed that some of my former students had traveled miles to come and had brought their parents with them. Two of them had brought their sweethearts. This always happens, old friends, students treasure your memory and you treasure theirs.

I think you're a mehboob, *if I could use an Urdu word, a sweetheart for a lot of people. Thank you very much.*

My pleasure.

NOTES

1   Edward W. Said, *The Pen and the Sword: Conversations with David Barsamian* (Monroe, Maine: Common Courage Press, 1994), p. 53.

2   Tim Weiner, "Raids Are Seen As One Battle In a Long Fight," *New York Times*, August 23, 1998, p. 1: 1.

3   Eqbal Ahmad, "Terrorism: Theirs and Ours," October 12, 1998. Available from Alternative Radio (see Appendix).

4   See Eqbal Ahmad and Richard J. Barnet, "A Reporter At Large: Bloody Games," *New Yorker*, April 11, 1988, pp. 44–86.

5   Richard Halloran, "U.S. May Establish Afghan Rebel Ties," *New York Times*, June 18, 1986, p. A8.

6   See James Risen, "To Bomb Sudan Plant, or Not: A Year Later, Debates Rankle," *New York Times*, October 27, 1999, p. A1.

7   Eqbal Ahmad, interview with David Barsamian, *The Progressive* 62: 11 (November 1998): 38.

8   See Idries Shah, *Sufism* (New York: Anchor Books, 1971).

9   Muhammad Iqbal, *Kulliyat-e-Iqbal* (Aligarh: India, 1975), p. 278. Translation by David Barsamian.

10 Iqbal, *Kulliyat-e-Iqbal*, p. 401. Trans. Barsamian.

11 Eqbal Ahmad, "The Neo-Fascist State: Notes on the Pathology of Power in the Third World," *Arab Studies Quarterly* 3: 2 (Spring 1981).

12 Taslima Nasrin, *Shame*, trans. Kankabati Datta (New York: Prometheus Books, 1997).

13 See Dexter Filkins, "Writer Risks Threats, Death on Her Return to Bangladesh," *Los Angeles Times*, November 13, 1998, p. A5.

14 Suzanne Goldenberg, "Pakistan PM to Impose Sharia," *The Guardian*, August 29, 1998, p. 13.

15 Paul Farrelly and Jonathan Calvert, "Pakistan PM Probed over 'Secret Fortune,'" *The Observer*, September 27, 1998, p. 1.

16 Barbara Crossette, "New Delhi Pledges to Sign World Ban on Nuclear Tests," *New York Times*, September 25, 1998, p. A1.

17 See Robert Fisk, "Curfew Shields Forces of Darkness," *The Independent*, July 19, 1993, p. 9; and Anthony Lewis, "Heartbreak House," *New York Times*, October 20, 1997, p. A19.

18 See Robert Fisk, "One Candle in the Heart of Darkness," *The Independent*, October 27, 1996, p. 14.

19 See Laura Silber and Allan Little, *Yugoslavia: Death of a Nation*, revised ed. (New York: Penguin, 1997), pp. 345–50.

20   See Philip Gourevitch, *We Wish to Inform You That Tomorrow We Will Be Killed with Our Families: Stories from Rwanda* (New York: St. Martin's Press, 1999).

21   Sigmund Freud, *Civilization and Its Discontents*, ed. and trans. James Strachey (New York: W.W. Norton, 1961), p. 72. See also Sigmund Freud, *Group Psychology and the Analysis of the Ego*, ed. and trans. James Strachey (New York: W.W. Norton, 1959), pp. 42–43.

22   Vandana Shiva, "Recovery of the Commons," Alternative Radio, September 25, 1994. Available from Alternative Radio (see Appendix). See also Vandana Shiva, *Biopiracy: The Plunder of Nature and Knowledge* (Boston: South End Press, 1997); and Vandana Shiva, *Stolen Harvest: The Hijacking of the Global Food Supply* (Cambridge: South End Press, 1999).

23   See page 124.

24   Antonio Gramsci, *Selections from the Prison Notebooks of Antonio Gramsci*, trans. and ed. Quintin Hoare and Geoffrey N. Smith (New York: International Publishers, 1990), p. 175.

25   Albert Camus, "Neither Victims Nor Executions," in *Between Hell and Reason: Essays from the Resistance Newspaper Combat, 1944–1947*, ed. and trans. Alexandre de Gramont (Hanover: Wesleyan University Press, 1991), pp. 115–40.

26   Iqbal, *Kulliyat-e-Iqbal*, p. 534. Trans. Barsamian.

SELECTED BIBLIOGRAPHY

EQBAL AHMAD

1964. "Trade Unionism." In *State and Society in Modern North Africa.* Ed. Carl Brown. Washington, DC: The Middle East Institute.

December 1964. "Tunisia's Trade Unions." *African Studies Bulletin.* Volume 7, Number 4, pp. 13ff.

August 30, 1965. "Revolutionary Warfare: How to Tell When the Rebels Have Won." The *Nation.* Volume 201, Number 5, pp. 95–100. Reprinted in *Revolutionary Warfare: How to Tell When the Rebels Have Won.* Boston: New England Free Press, 1965. Also printed in *Viet Nam: History, Documents, and Opinions on a Major World Crisis.* Ed. Marvin E. Gettleman. Greenwich: Fawcett Premier, 1965, pp. 351–62.

1966. "Trade Unionism in the Maghreb." In *State and Society in Independent North Africa.* Ed. L. Carl Brown. Washington, DC: Middle East Institute.

1968. Dialogue with Samuel P. Huntington et al. In *No More Vietnams? The War and the Future of American Policy.* Ed. Richard M. Pfeffer. New York: Harper and Row.

January 29, 1968. "Primer for Revolutionary Guerrillas." The *Nation.* Volume 206, Number 5, pp. 149–153.

July–August 1968. "Radical But Wrong." *Monthly Review.* Volume 20, Number 23, pp. 70–83. Reprinted in *Régis Debray and the Latin American Revolution.* Eds. Paul Sweezy and Leo Huberman. New York: Monthly Review Press, 1969, pp. 70–83.

March 3, 1969. "America as Superpower: How We Look to the Third World." The *Nation.* Volume 208, Number 9, pp. 265–269.

1971. Foreword to *The June 1967 Arab–Israeli War: Miscalculation or Conspiracy?* Ed. Samò Elias. Wilmette, Illinois: Medina University Press.

1971. "Revolutionary Warfare and Counterinsurgency." In *National Liberation: Revolution in the Third World.* Eds. Norman Miller and Roderick Aya. New York: Free Press, pp. 137–213.

February 1971. "Theories of Counterinsurgency." *Bulletin of Concerned Asian Scholars.* Volume 3, Number 2, pp. 76–80.

August 2, 1971. "Winning Hearts and Minds: The Theory and Fallacies of Counterinsurgency." The *Nation.* Volume 213, Number 3, pp. 70–85.

September 2, 1971. "Letter to a Pakistani Diplomat." *The New York Review of Books.* Volume 17, Number 3.

Winter 1972. "Notes on South Asia in Crisis." *Bulletin of Concerned Asian Scholars.* Volume 4, Number 1, pp. 23–29.

February 1972. "Speaking Truth to Power: An Interview with Daniel Ellsberg, Tony Russo, and Eqbal Ahmad." Interview by Studs Terkel. *Harper's Magazine.* Volume 244, Number 1461, pp. 52ff.

July 1973. "South Asia in Crisis and India's Counterinsurgency War Against the Nagas and Mizos." *Bulletin of Concerned Asian Scholars.* Volume 5, Number 1, pages 25–36.

1974. "Pakistan: Signposts to a Police State." *Journal of Contemporary Asia.* Volume 4, Number 4.

March 1974. "America and Russia in South Asia: Conflict or Collusion?" *Bulletin of Concerned Asian Scholars.* Volume 6, Number 1, pp. 22–27.

1975. "The Economic Implications of U.S. Foreign Policy." With Cyril E. Black et al. Sound recording. Santa Barbara: California Center for the Study of Democratic Insitutions.

1975. "'A World Restored' Revisited: American Diplomacy in the Middle East." In *Middle East Crucible: Studies on the Arab–Israeli War of October 1973.* Ed. Naseer H. Aruri. Wilmette, Illinois: Medina University Press.

Winter 1978. "M'hamed Ali and the Tunisian Labor Movement." With Stuart Schaar. *Race and Class.* Volume 19, Number 3, pp. 253–76.

1978. "Indictment for Conspiracy to Murder Orlando Letelier." *Race and Class.* Volume 19, Number 3.

May 1978. "Human Rights in Morocco and Tunisia." With Stuart Schaar. *MERIP Report.* Volume 8, Number 4.

Summer 1979. "The Iranian Revolution." *Race and Class*. Volume 21, Number 1, pp. 3–11.

1980. Eqbal Ahmad, "Political Culture and Foreign Policy: Notes on American Interventions in the Third World." In *For Better or Worse: The American Influence in the World*. Ed. Allen Freeman Davis. Westport, Connecticut: Greenwood Press, pp. 119–31.

March 3, 1980. "Iran and the West: A Century of Subjugation." *Christianity and Crisis*. Volume 40, pp. 37–44.

Summer 1980. "A Perspective from the Third World on War and Its Abolition." Interviewed by Virginia Heiseman. *Race and Class*. Volume 22, Number 1, pp. 77–81.

Summer 1980. "From Potato Sack to Potato Mash: The Contemporary Crisis of the Third World." *Arab Studies Quarterly*. Volume 2, Number 3, pp. 223ff.

Summer 1980. "The Question of Palestine" Review of Edward W. Said, *The Question of Palestine*. *Race and Class*. Volume 22, Number 1, pp. 85–91.

Autumn 1980. "Pakistan in Crisis: An Interview with Eqbal Ahmad." *Race and Class*. Volume 22, Number 2, pp. 129–46.

Fall 1980. "Post-Colonial Systems of Power." *Arab Studies Quarterly*. Volume 2, Number 4, pp. 350ff.

Spring 1981. "The Neo-Fascist State: Notes on the Pathology of Power in the Third World." *Arab Studies Quarterly*. Volume 3, Number 2, pp. 170–80.

1982. "Rentier State and Shia Islam in the Iranian Revolution—Comments." *Theory and Society*. Volume 11, Number 3, pp. 293–300.

March 1983. "The Public Relations of Ethnocide." *Journal of Palestine Studies*. Volume 12, pp. 31–40.

Spring 1983. "Introduction." In *The Invasion of Lebanon*. Special double issue of *Race and Class*. Eds. Eqbal Ahmad and Ibrahim Abu-Lughod. Volume 24, Number 4, pp. i–viii.

Spring 1984. "'Pioneering' in the Nuclear Age: An Essay on Israel and the Palestinians." *Race and Class*. Volume 25, Number 4, pp. 1–20.

1984. "Islam and Politics." In *Islamic Impact*. Eds. Yvonne Yazbeck Haddad, Byron Haines, and Ellison Banks Findly. New York: Syracuse University Press, pp. 7–26.

1985. "Cracks in the Western World(view)." *Radical America*. Volume 19, Number 1, pp. 37–46.

1985. "Islam and Politics." In *Islam, Politics, and the State: The Pakistan Experience*. Ed. Mohammad Ashgar Khan. London: Zed Books.

September 21, 1985. "Only as Good as Its Members." The *Nation*. Volume 241, Number 8, pp. 242–44.

May–June 1986. "Comprehending Terror." *Middle East Report*. Volume 16, Number 3, pp. 3–5.

April 11, 1988. "A Reporter At Large: Bloody Games." With Richard J. Barnet. *New Yorker*, pp. 44–86.

May–June 1989. "Middle East Peace Priorities in the US: Seven Perspectives." With Noam Chomsky et al. *Middle East Report*. Volume 19, Number 3.

July 1990. "Kashmir and Its Challenges." *Pakistan Horizon*. Volume 43, Number 3, pp. 11–20.

August 1990. "An Era of Grief: United States Policy in the Middle East Created a Power Vacuum that Saddam Hussein Has Moved to Fill." *New Statesman and Society*. Volume 3, pp. 12–13.

1991. "What Arabs Know, and You Don't." In *Gulf War: Views from the Other Side*. Manila: Socio-Pastoral Institute.

1991. "Portent of a New Century." In *Beyond the Storm: A Gulf Crisis Reader*. Eds. Phyllis Bennis and Michel Moushabeck. Brooklyn: Olive Branch Press.

March–April 1991. "Nightmare Victory?" *Mother Jones*. Volume 16, Number 2, pp. 4–7.

March 17, 1991. "The Hundred-Hour War." *Dawn*. Volume 50, Number 76, p. 11.

June 1991. "Soul Struggles," *New Statesman and Society*. Volume 4, pp. 23–24.

1993. "Racism and the State: The Coming Crisis of U.S.-Japanese Relations." In *Japan in the World*. Eds. Masao Miyoshi and H.D. Harootunian. Durham: Duke UP, pp. 40–48.

1993. "M'Hamed Ali: Tunisian Labor Organizer." In *Struggle and Survival in the Modern Middle East*. With Stuart Schaar. Ed. Edmund Burke III. Berkeley: UC Berkeley Press, pp. 253–76. Revised version of article from *Race and Class*, Winter 1978.

Summer 1993. "At the Cold War's End: A World of Pain." *Boston Review*. Volume 18, Numbers 3–4.

1994. Introduction to *The Pen and the Sword: Conversations with Edward W. Said.* Ed. David Barsamian. Monroe, Maine: Common Courage Press.

June 8, 1997. "Culture of Imperialism." *Dawn.* Volume 50, Number 152, p. 13.

September 23, 1997. "Algeria's Unending Tragedy." *Dawn.* Volume 50, Number 257, p. 13.

February 2, 1998. "Feudal Culture and Violence (Roots of Violence in Pakistan) II." *Dawn.* Volume 52, Number 31, p. 13.

Spring 1998. "Jihad International, Inc." *CovertAction Quarterly.* Number 64, pp. 29–32.

May 17, 1998. "India's Obsession, Our Choice." *Dawn.* Volume 52, Number 130, p. 13.

June 6, 1998. "Reason as Spectator." *Dawn.* Volume 52, Number 151, p. 13.

June 28, 1998. "No Alternative to Dialogue." *Dawn.* Volume 52, Number 172, p. 13.

June 29, 1998. "Fire on the Mountain." The *Nation.* Volume 266, Number 23, p. 6.

August 27–September 2, 1998. "A Mirage Misnamed Strategic Depth." *Al-Ahram Weekly* (Egypt).

September 21, 1998. "Missile Diplomacy." The *Nation.* Volume 267, Number 8, p. 29.

November 5–11, 1998. "After the Peace of the Weak." *Al-Ahram Weekly* (Egypt). Number 402.

1999. "When Mountains Die." In *Pakistan-India Nuclear Peace Reader.* Lahore, Pakistan: Mashal, pp. 8–13.

INDEX

APPENDIX

Recordings of Eqbal Ahmad
from Alternative Radio

Intellectuals, Ideology, and the State (Cambridge, MA, October 16, 1998)

Terrorism: Theirs and Ours (Boulder, CO, October 12, 1998)

The Boulder Interviews (Boulder, CO, October 12, 1998)

Distorted Histories (Amherst, MA, August 24, 1998)

The Amherst Interviews (Amherst, MA, December 14, 1996)

From Bandung to Mexico: The Decline of the Third World (Boulder, CO, March 22, 1995)

Islam, Arab Middle East, Israel, etc. (Boulder, CO, August 11, 1993)

India, Pakistan, Afghanistan (Boulder, CO, August 4, 1993)

Portents of a New Century (Madison, WI, October 17, 1991)

On the Eve of the Gulf War (New York, NY, January 13, 1991)

Roots of the Gulf Crisis (Boston, MA, November 17, 1990)

Third World Dependency (New York, NY, December 26, 1983)

About Alternative Radio

Alternative Radio, established in 1986, is an award-winning weekly one-hour public affairs program offered free to all public radio stations in the United States, Canada, Europe, and beyond. AR provides information, analyses, and views that are frequently ignored or distorted in corporate media. With headquarters based in Boulder, Colorado, and with only three paid staff, AR airs on nearly 200 radio stations. Visit our website at www.alternativeradio.org.

About Haymarket Books

Haymarket Books is a nonprofit, progressive book distributor and publisher, a project of the Center for Economic Research and Social Change. We believe that activists need to take ideas, history, and politics into the many struggles for social justice today. Learning the lessons of past victories, as well as defeats, can arm a new generation of fighters for a better world. As Karl Marx said, "The philosophers have merely interpreted the world; the point, however, is to change it."

We take inspiration and courage from our namesakes, the Haymarket Martyrs, who gave their lives fighting for a better world. Their 1886 struggle for the eight-hour day, which gave us May Day, the international workers' holiday, reminds workers around the world that ordinary people can organize and struggle for their own liberation. These struggles continue today across the globe-struggles against oppression, exploitation, hunger, and poverty.

It was August Spies, one of the Martyrs targeted for being an immigrant and an anarchist, who predicted the battles being fought to this day. "If you think that by hanging us you can stamp out the labor movement," Spies told the judge, "then hang us. Here you will tread upon a spark, but here, and there, and behind you, and in front of you, and everywhere, the flames will blaze up. It is a subterranean fire. You cannot put it out. The ground is on fire upon which you stand."

We could not succeed in our publishing efforts without the generous financial support of our readers. Many people contribute to our project through the Haymarket Sustainers program, where donors receive free books in return for their monetary support. If you would like to be a part of this program, please contact us at info@haymarketbooks.org.

Shop our full catalog online at www.haymarketbooks.org or call 773-583-7884.

About the Authors

Eqbal Ahmad (1933–1999) was a Pakistani political scientist, writer, journalist, and anti-war activist. A prolific writer and journalist, Eqbal was widely consulted by revolutionaries, journalists, activist leaders and policymakers around the world. He was an editor of the journal *Race and Class*, contributing editor of *Middle East Report* and *L'Economiste du Tiers Monde*, co-founder of Pakistan Forum, and an editorial board member of *Arab Studies Quarterly*. Upon his retirement from Hampshire College in 1997, he settled permanently in Pakistan, where he continued to write a weekly column for *Dawn*, Pakistan's oldest English language newspaper.

One of America's most tireless and wide-ranging investigative journalists, David Barsamian has altered the independent media landscape, both with his weekly radio show Alternative Radio—now in its 30th year—and his books with Noam Chomsky, Howard Zinn, Tariq Ali, Arundhati Roy and Edward Said.

Edward W. Said (1935–2003) was University Professor of English and Comparative Literature at Columbia University. A member of the American Academy of Arts and Sciences, the Royal Society of Literature and of Kings College Cambridge, his celebrated works include *Orientalism*, *The End of the Peace Process*, *Power, Politics and Culture*, and the memoir *Out of Place*. He is also the editor, with Christopher Hitchens, of *Blaming the Victims*, published by Verso.

Pervez Hoodbhoy has taught in the physics department at Quaid-e-Azam University in Islamabad for 40 years and now also teaches at Forman Christian College in Lahore. He has won many awards, including the Abdus Salam Award for Mathematics, the Book of the Year Award from the National Book Council of Pakistan, and UNESCO's Kalinga Prize for science popularization. In addition to producing many documentaries for Pakistani television, he has written the books *Islam and Science: Religious Orthodoxy and the Battle for Rationality*, *Education and the State: Fifty Years of Pakistan*, and *Confronting the Bomb: Pakistani and Indian Scientists Speak Out*.

Printed in the USA
CPSIA information can be obtained
at www.ICGtesting.com
JSHW022007270524
63683JS00003B/7